Fifty Years
of American Drama
1900-1950

TWENTIETH-CENTURY LITERATURE IN AMERICA

GENERAL EDITORS

WILLIAM VAN O'CONNOR, PH.D.
University of Minnesota

FREDERICK J. HOFFMAN, PH.D.
University of Wisconsin

Fifty Years of American Drama, 1900–1950
by ALAN S. DOWNER, *of Princeton University*

The Modern Novel in America, 1900–1950
by FREDERICK J. HOFFMAN

Achievement in American Poetry, 1900–1950
by LOUISE BOGAN, *poet and critic*

TO BE PUBLISHED IN SPRING 1952

The Rise of Short Fiction in America,
1900–1950
by RAY B. WEST, JR., *of the University of Iowa*

An Age of Criticism, 1900–1950
by WILLIAM VAN O'CONNOR

Men, Ideas, and Judgments:
American Non-Fiction, 1900–1950
by MAY BRODBECK, *of the University of Minnesota*
JAMES GRAY, *of the University of Minnesota*
WALTER METZGER, *of Columbia University*

Fifty Years
of American Drama

1900-1950

༺༗༻

Alan S. Downer

Princeton University

HENRY REGNERY COMPANY

CHICAGO: 1951

Copyright 1951

HENRY REGNERY COMPANY

Chicago 4, Illinois

Manufactured in the United States of America

PREFACE

A SMALL BOOK on a large subject requires an apology. The following essay is not intended as a history of the American Drama in its most productive years. Rather it is an attempt to analyze the product: where it came from, how it developed, and where it arrived. It involves, therefore, the inclusion of plays of varying worth, and the omission of many of both historical interest and aesthetic value.

I have written in terms of plays rather than playwrights, since my interest is in dramatic art rather than individual achievement. The word American appears inevitably many times; it is to be understood not in its jingoistic sense, but rather as it describes an art which has grown out of a people and its concerns, as a theater asserting its independence of transatlantic forms and conventions. Many of the now-forgotten earlier plays of the period are discussed at what would be disproportionate length were it not that some familiarity with them is necessary to establish a point of departure. The chapter divisions may seem arbitrary; they are intended to organize the material in terms of dramatic form (representational and presentational) and of subject matter (folk drama and comedy) most typical of America. The omission of any consideration of musical comedy is certainly arbitrary, but, like the motion picture, it deserves a book of its own.

For a fuller historical treatment the reader should turn to the works cited in the list of Suggested Readings.

A.S.D.

CONTENTS

Fifty Years
of American Drama

I

THEATRICALISM

As early as 1900 New York City became the center of American theatrical production. There were still managers and famous actors and stock companies that confined their activities to Boston, Chicago, and other large communities, but in general the members of the profession were beginning to measure success in terms of the New York box office, to manufacture plays in terms of the tastes of the New York audience. They referred to the rest of the nation as "The Road," where plays were whipped into shape before meeting the supreme test of a New York first night, or where successful plays might be taken to reap the harvest of their New York reputation.

Of some twenty-six works playing at the legitimate theaters in New York during the first week of 1900, thirteen might be considered in a study of American drama. They included two new plays by the prolific Clyde Fitch, *Barbara Fritchie* in which Julia Marlowe was starring for the eleventh week, and *The Cowboy and the Lady* just beginning its second week with Nat C. Goodwin and Maxine Elliott. *Ben Hur* was in its sixth week and William Gillette, starring in his celebrated version of *Sherlock Holmes,* in his ninth. If the latter play must be discounted as alien in subject, it might be counterbalanced by James A. Herne's folksy perennial, *Shore Acres,* or the belligerently native *Way Down East,* which had seven weeks behind it, or the totally forgotten, unashamedly melodramatic *Wheels Within Wheels, The Village Postmaster, The Bowery After Dark,* and *Because She Loved Him So.* Richard Mansfield, the leading actor of the day, was presenting a repertory which included, for the week, *Arms and the Man* and *The Devil's Disciple, Cyrano de Bergerac, Dr. Jekyll and Mr. Hyde,* and one "American" play, *Beau Brummel,* an apprentice work of the ubiquitous Fitch. Probably the brightest, most "American," and most vital theatrical evening of the week was to be found at Weber and Fields' Music Hall, where Fitch's historical romance was being roasted as *Barbara Fidgety.*

Out on the road, audiences were applauding or were about to applaud *Davy Crockett, Rip Van Winkle, Across the Pacific, The Still Alarm, Hearts of the Blue Ridge,* and the never-fading excitement of James O'Neill as the *Count of Monte Cristo,* triumphantly standing on his pasteboard rock to proclaim that the world was his.

Few of these plays, of course, are of concern to any but the most devoted historian of the drama. A brief consideration of their general characteristics may, however, be in order as a prelude to the significant works to come. Without exception these plays are shaped to the talents of the actor and exploit the possibilities of the physical theater. These are, to be sure, legitimate if limited methods of stimulating an audience. One recalls, for instance, William Gillette's incarnation of Conan Doyle's detective. Gillette was a spare, thin-faced man belonging to what was called "the repressed school" of acting. Consequently he directed his fellow performers to behave on the stage as if they were walking on a red-hot griddle, while he himself moved quietly and with dignity through the hectic proceedings and was vastly acclaimed by enraptured audiences. The ending of the third act of *Sherlock Holmes,* devised by Gillette for his own talents, was the sheerest theatrical trickery. Holmes and his assistant are trapped by the villains in a stone dungeon. Suddenly the lights go out and nothing can be seen but the red glow of the detective's cigar. In the dark, the villains are heard rushing across the stage as the red glow moves slowly down stage to the far right. As they surround it, the lights suddenly flash on: the villains are clustered at right around a cigar, burning by itself on a window ledge. Holmes and his assistant, standing by a door at the back of the stage, bid them good night and make a hasty exit.

Clyde Fitch was famous for his ability to provide leading actors with roles which would exploit their attractive idiosyncrasies. *Beau Brummel* was tailored to the half-classical, half-romantic genius of Mansfield, as *The Cowboy and the Lady* made use in carefully balanced scenes of the romantic charms of Mr. Goodwin and Miss Elliott. *Ben Hur* is widely remembered for the mechanical ingenuity of its chariot race, while the great moment of *Davy Crockett* came as the simple woodsman protected his sweetheart from the wolf pack by thrusting his arm into the door sockets in place of a missing bar.

Such limitation, restricting the dramatist's art to the exploitation of the actor and stage machinery, was self-imposed by the members of the theatrical profession who frankly believed they were giving the public what it demanded. And even admitting the limitation, the American theater at the turn of the twentieth century had made one small step forward. From the days of its origin until well into the nineteenth century it had been bound to the subject matter and was imitative of the conventions of the English stage. But the somewhat timid Americanism of such late nineteenth-century playwrights as Bronson Howard (*Shenandoah*, 1889) and Augustus Thomas (*Alabama*, 1891), and the remarkable originality of James A. Herne (*Margaret Fleming*, 1890; *Shore Acres*, 1892) contributed to the first liberation of the theater, breaking some of the bonds that had held it to the past, specifically to the English stage.

The effect of this liberation is shown chiefly in the choice of setting, in the characters employed, and to some extent in the language of many celebrated plays of the first decades of the twentieth century. In the situations and the general tendency of the action there is still little difference between the chief works of American playwrights and those of such successful English dramatists as Arthur Wing Pinero and Henry Arthur Jones.

It was certainly the continued American interest in Japan, dating from the visit of Admiral Perry, that led to the staging of John Luther Long's novelette, *Madame Butterfly*. But it was the proved power of the deserted mistress to draw tears that led David Belasco to collaborate with Mr. Long in the dramatization. Described as "an exotic romance," the one-act play employs a few typical Japanese conventions, the geisha, the marriage broker, hara-kiri, but many more conventions of the theater-at-large. Cho-Cho-San had lived for three months, in her professional capacity, with Lieutenant B. F. Pinkerton, U. S. N. Although he treated the relationship as a commercial transaction, the power of love forced Butterfly to regard it as a true marriage. After his departure on stateside leave, despite the importunities of a wealthy merchant and the machinations of a marriage broker, she remained true to Pinkerton and taught their baby daughter, Trouble, to wave the American flag. The play begins the spring following the separation of the lovers, with Butterfly awaiting Pinkerton's return. But he has married in the States and brings his wife to Japan. She visits Butterfly to console her and offers to adopt the child, but to the ex-geisha her love is her honor. The curtain falls as she commits hara-kiri with her father's sword on which is inscribed the Japanese sentiment, "To die with honor . . . when one can no longer live with honor."

The power of this small play to awaken the sympathy of audiences was demonstrated not only by its immediate success in New York and London, but by its reincarnation as the libretto for Puccini's celebrated opera. But the power is a *theatrical* power, depending on the charm of the leading lady and her knowledge of the tricks of her art. The situation itself is neither tragic nor exotic; it has served the theater of all nations and playwrights of every caliber from Terence in ancient Roman comedy to Dion Boucicault in nineteenth-century English melodrama. Belasco and Long have simply draped it in a kimono and painted almond eyes on the star.

However, the New York audiences that first sat before the play in March 1900, must have felt thoroughly at home with more than the situation. Butterfly and her maid talk English, but it is the English of the "Japanese Schoolboy," the once popular comic figure, Hashimura Togo; there can be no doubt of the intended reaction to such a passage as this:

BUTTERFLY. O look! Suzuki—a robins, the fir' these Spring! Go, see if he's stay for nes'.

SUZUKI. It *is* a robins, O Cho-Cho-San! . . . But he's fly away.

BUTTERFLY. O! How they are slow this year! Sa-ey, see if you don' fin' one tha's more in-dus-trial and domestics.

SUZUKI. There are none yet.

BUTTERFLY. But soon they nes' now. Suzuki, w'en we see that ship comin' in—sa-ey—then we goin' put flowers aevery where, an' if it's night, we goin' hang up mos' one thousand lanterns—eh-ha?

SUZUKI. Not got moaney for thousan'.

BUTTERFLY. Wael, twenty, mebby; an' sa-ey w'en we see him comin' quick up path—*(imitates)* so-so-so—*(lifts her kimono and strides in masculine fashion)* to look for liddle wive—me—me jus' goin' hide behind shoji *(making two holes with her wet finger in the low paper shoji and peeping through)* an' watch an' make believe me gone 'way; leave liddle note—sayin': "Goon-bye, sayonara, Butterfly." . . . Now he come in. . . . *(Hides)* Ah! An' then he get angry! An' he say all kinds of 'Merican languages—debbils—hells! But before he get too angry, me run out and flew aroun' his neck! *(She illustrates with Suzuki, who is carried away, and embraces her with fervor)* Sa-ey! *You* no flew roun' his neck—jus' me!

The effectiveness of such a scene depends upon two things: the snob appeal of foreign attempts to speak English, and the awkward charm of the soubrette's imitation of masculine behavior. They have been so often used that the laughter they evoke is easy, not thoughtful. Easy, too, the irony in the visit of the American consul to Butterfly. Expecting that he has only to put an end to a commercial association, he is unable to tell her (as he has already informed the spectators) that Pinkerton is not really her husband. When she speaks of "making smash," the consul points out to the audience that this is Pinkerton's slang, and when she winks behind her fan, it is "Pinkerton's very wink!" Such asides serve to italicize the plainest of ironies; they are the stock-in-trade of hack writers of the crudest melodrama.

The hand of Mr. Belasco, with his delight in the mechanics of production, is to be seen in the device by which the passing of time and the devotion of Madame Butterfly are represented. Spying Pinkerton's ship in the harbor, she calls Suzuki and Trouble to watch with her, forming a "picture."

During the vigil, the night comes on. Suzuki lights the floor lamps, the stars come out, the dawn breaks, the floor lights flicker out one by one, the birds begin to sing, and the day discovers Suzuki and the baby fast asleep on the floor; but Madame Butterfly is awake, still watching, her face white and strained.

Again, the intention is to exploit the possibilities of the theater, and the pleasure derived is a delight in the mechanical imitation of natural phenomena. The hocus-pocus of lights and dimmers simply repeats what the precedent action and dialogue have already made abundantly clear.

In sum, considered as dramatic art, *Madame Butterfly* is an example of complete theatricalism, creating emotional pleasure for its audiences out of an unreal situation with stereotyped characters and a setting, exotic in the sense that it has been made to look, superficially, unfamiliar. Its effect is instantaneous and temporary. There is nothing in it to trouble the spectator with serious questions about human nature, ethics, or morality, or even the more obvious problems of prostitution and race relations.

Belasco was recognized in his own time as primarily a wizard of the stage. On the other hand, the untimely death of Clyde Fitch was commonly said to have cut off the one writer who might have produced the "Great American Drama." Fitch had, it is true, worked zealously in many styles in his few years in the theater and scarcely a season passed in the early years of the century without at least two of his plays competing vigorously for the entertainment dollars of New Yorkers. He was acclaimed for the power of his characterization, the freshness of his themes, and the frankness of his dialogue. Indeed for the last he was not infrequently reproached.

Madame Butterfly was described as "exotic romance"; Fitch's *The Girl with the Green Eyes* (1902) has been classified as "drama of human character" and "social comedy." Since human character and society are unequalled subjects for comedy, it will be useful to behold what Fitch does with them. His focus, as the title indicates, is on a jealous woman and the very nearly fatal ending of her marriage because of her determination to view all suspicious circumstances through a distorting glass. Certainly Fitch has been generous in providing circumstances for her to distort. The married life of Jinny Austin really consumes only a minor part of the action of the play. The complexity of the plot requires Fitch to devote long scenes to revealing that Jinny's wastrel brother, Geoff, is, unknown to her, a bigamist; that her good friend, Ruth, is secretly married to her brother; that her husband, in the way of business, must straighten out Geoff's and Ruth's tangled lives.

The cards are stacked against Jinny from the start. Her husband is bound to secrecy by Ruth (so he cannot explain to Jinny that there is nothing wrong in their relationship), Ruth is bound to secrecy by Geoff (so she cannot tell Jinny of her marriage and thus justify Austin's actions), then Austin is sworn to secrecy by Geoff (so he cannot explain to Jinny about her brother's earlier marriage to the housemaid), and finally Jinny makes her husband swear to help her beloved brother, no matter what may be involved. Austin, of course, is one of Theater's (if not Nature's) Noblemen who will not break a vow even to save his own marriage or his wife's sanity. And all these vows of honor and oaths of secrecy are the motives and cues for the action of this "drama of human character." Just, one should add, as they had been for uncounted sensation dramas of the popular theaters of the nineteenth century.

As acted by Clara Bloodgood, Jinny took on the appearance of an enormously vital woman driven almost to madness by a "tragic flaw" in her character. Jinny recognizes her own flaw and is ashamed of her nickname, "The Girl with the Green Eyes," but, as she points out, she has inherited a jealous disposition from her parents and there is nothing she can do about it. It hardly seems possible that a man-of-the-New-World like Fitch could subscribe to such medieval notions of psychology and human motivation, unless—as one must conclude from a study of the play—he learned about humanity from the theater. Jinny, it is plain, is a humour character, in the Elizabethan sense of the word. The elements are so mixed in her that her sole motivating force, over which she can exercise no control, is jealousy. To reinforce such a conclusion about Fitch's antique method of characterization there are several minor humours in the play. Jinny's father, for instance, appears several times, but always to demonstrate his humour—that

cigars are a panacea for every critical situation, physical
or emotional. An even more obvious humour is Peter Cunningham, a young man in the best of health, who doses
himself with a variety of pills on an elaborate schedule. A
combination of one-dimensional characters and an artificial intrigue makes for excellent farce, but hardly for social
satire or drama of character. Indeed, it becomes evident,
all this vowing and giving in secrecy exists with the sole
aim of a resounding curtain for Act III in which the
heroine is struck down by the revelation of one after another piece of stubbornly concealed truth. Here Ruth, at
the end of her passage of truth-telling, turns upon the
madly jealous Jinny with,

> To spare me, and above all to spare you the knowledge of
> your brother's sin, your husband has kept Geoffrey's secret from
> you. You have *well* repaid him!

And so, of course, say the spectators, for they like Austin,
have been in on all the secrets from the beginning. That
Jinny might have more justification than a hereditary flaw
for becoming suspicious in the presence of so much
mysterious machination and concealed crime is an unraised
issue. There is more than a little sadism in the playwright's
apparent seriousness in torturing the Girl with the Green
Eyes.

Apart from the characterization and the plotting there
are other aspects of an older theatricalism in the play.
Fitch twice makes use of extended soliloquies, once to
allow Jinny to explain to the audience her increasing
jealousy of her husband, as if the action could not be trusted
to convey it, and once to allow Jinny an emotional purge
before attempting suicide. If the first of these may be jus-

tified as necessary exposition for the slow-witted, the second has no dramatic function. It exploits emotion for its own sake without revealing any deeper aspects of the heroine's character, or advancing the action, or clarifying the theme. Fitch has made it apparent from the start that he is against jealousy, that faith is essential for a happy marriage, and that his heroine is strong only in her greatest weakness. To watch her voluble preparations for suicide is too much of a not very good thing.

Wherein then is the clue to the contemporary success of the play? Perhaps it may be suggested by Jinny's rueful confession: "I want to be Brunnhilde and I'm only Frou Frou." Even the heroine conceives of herself, not as a human being, but as a character in a play. Her behavior in a sense bears this out. When her husband is first angry with her because of her irrational jealousy, she charms him back to good humor by performing a "regular skirt dance" to the Floradora Sextette played on a pianola. This crude exploitation of her femininity might be compared to Nora's tarantella in *A Doll's House*. In both instances womanly wiles are used to distract husbands from consideration of a most serious subject. In Ibsen, the action was intended to strengthen his theme that women were treated not as individuals but as slaves or toys. Fitch, however, looks benignly upon Jinny's dance: at this moment she redeems herself, temporarily, for the unhappiness caused by her unfortunate humour. It is enough for Fitch that Jinny has been provided with a theatrically effective situation. He refuses to recognize the ethical or social issue which might weaken the excitement of his plot while enlarging the dimensions of his play. And there is no question that the majority of his spectators were grateful for his control, or his blindness.

They were grateful, too, for his comic sense. Mr. Till-man and his cigars, Peter Cunningham and his pills are an easy form of humor. So too are such epigrams as, "mas-culine ballast is the only kind that's safe if you want to make life's journey in a love balloon," a kind of up-to-the-minute proverbial wisdom that loses its crispness as time moves on and, in this instance, acquires sinister over-tones that Fitch never intended. But the best comedy of the play is found in the second act, which takes place before the statue of the Apollo Belvedere in the Vatican. Here the progress of the main action is regularly inter-rupted by a series of tourists, French, German, and American, who pass through and comment on the statue. The scene attests Fitch's close observation of human be-havior and only increases the regret that he could not shake off the collar of theatricalism in connection with his major characters and their problems. As it stands, however, this excellent comic scene is little better than a skit, a vaude-ville sketch, since it is really irrelevant to the play as a whole, introducing characters otherwise unconnected with the plot, and forcing the plot characters to make jokes about undraped statuary instead of sticking to their business.

The Girl with the Green Eyes is artificial, devised to amuse, excite, and move, but not to trouble an audience. The same intentions control *The City* (1909), Fitch's strongest play, which differs from *The Girl* mainly in the immediacy of its theme. In *The City* Fitch treats a twen-tieth-century phenomenon, the increasing desertion of the American village for the American metropolis, and the effect of the shift on human character. *The City* is the story of George Rand, Jr., a young man of high character and unimpeachable ideals, who moves to New York and, under the pressure of political ambition, adopts the principle

that the end justifies the means. To attain the governor-
ship he sacrifices both his ideals and his human feeling; he
is even tempted to allow his sister to marry a blackguard,
since any effort to prevent the union would put a stop to
his ambitions. George is convinced, and the action of the
play seems to support him, that the code of the City destroys
character.

[In New York, he says:] You know one thing to perfection—
but only one—where your interests are centered! All city men
specialize—they have to *get* success and *keep* it! Every walk of
life, there, is a marathon! But the worst of it is, the goal isn't
stationary. It's like the horizon,—no man can reach it!

There is, to be sure, a certain contemporaneity about
the play. George's political nickname is "Teddy, Jr.," and
there are passing references to reform and trust-busting.
But the play is not so much timely as timeless, in the sense
that most theatricality is timeless. The real motive power
for the action is provided by the hero's sense of family
honor—he cannot bring himself to disclose the truth about
an indiscretion his father committed years ago, and this
antique and theatrical motive forces endless complications
upon the other situations in the plot, involving such sensational elements as illegitimacy, drug addiction, and incest.
The whole is expressed so awkwardly that it forever
recalls the worst moments of the older popular drama.
Hannock, Rand senior's bastard, is the stereotyped villain
of melodrama, who does not blush to declare to Rand
junior:

I knew your father was dishonest, and I told him that day;
I guess it killed him. And I've watched you and tempted you,
and helped you go on with his method! Every bit of this will

come out in my trial. I'll get a clever enough lawyer to manage *that!* And you'll lose, not only your ambition, but your position in the world, and one thing more besides,—the *woman* you're in love with!

Even Iago and Richard III could not have been more frank about their determination to prove villains, but they at least were permitted to declare their intentions in soliloquy rather than face to face with their victims. More particularly, they were not characters in a drama which pretended to be a realistic picture of contemporary life.

Hannock's speech is the stuff of melodrama. Audiences had long been accustomed to the confrontation of the hero and the villain accompanied, for the benefit of the careless spectator, by the villain's careful statement of his motives and methods. They had long been accustomed, also, to such easy comedy as Cicely's reply to her father's inquiry: "Who's that talking to your mother?"

CICELY: One of Middleburg's Social Queens, Mrs. Mulholland—known in our society as the lady who can wear a décolleté gown, cut in accordance with the Middleburg limit, and not look as if she'd dressed in a hurry and forgotten her collar!

It is true that wit, and especially satirical wit, is bound to be artificial; but in the most artificial comedies, of Congreve, Sheridan, Wilde, the wit is at least functional, generally serving to prepare the audience for the appearance of new characters. Mrs. Mulholland never enters in *The City;* she exists for the sake of a joke, of a gag, in short, for a moment of good theater.

A moment of good theater is also the excuse for the completely unnecessary death of the soubrette. George's sister, Cicely, has fallen in love with his bastard brother,

Hannock. George, who has not revealed the truth about their kinship because of his "sense of honor," is finally driven by the threat of incest to speak out.

> GEORGE. Cicely, are you strong? Are you brave? You must hear something *unbelievably terrible!*
> HANNOCK. Come along, don't listen to him!
> GEORGE. You *can't!*
> CICELY. I *will!* Leave go of me!
> GEORGE. My poor child, he's your . . .
> (HANNOCK, *without warning, pulls out a pistol from his hip pocket, and shoots her dead in* GEORGE's *arms*)

The shock of this unprepared action must have been so great that the audience had no time to analyze what had happened. But even hasty contemplation would have revealed that Cicely's death was due less to Hannock's gun than to George's stupidity in hiding the truth.

The truth was not in Fitch, nor in the theater for which he wrote. After the turmoil of his metropolitan career, George Rand can, in contrast to his earlier attitude, point out:

> Don't blame the City. It's not her fault! It's our own! What the City does is to bring out what's strongest in us. If at heart we're good, the good in us will win. If the bad is strongest, God help us! Don't blame the City! *She* gives the man his opportunity; it is up to *him* what he makes of it!

Doubtless this is a sentiment of immediate comfort to the New Yorkers for whom it was written—but a sentiment imposed from outside, from the box office, not growing out of the action of the play.

So too the concluding speech, as the heroine says to the dishonored and outcast George:

The man who has done wrong, and can own it up—face life all over again empty-handed, emptying his own hands of his own accord, turn his back on everything he counted on and lived for, because it is the right thing to do, and because—leaving the world out of it—*he had to be honest with himself!*—that—George—is the man I look up to ten times more than the one who was *born* good and lived good because he was never tempted to enjoy the spoils of going wrong!

The spectator who had not been inundated by Fitch's rhetoric and melodramatics might be inclined to ask what such a speech had to do with the case of the hero. It is the dramatist speaking, not the character.

Fitch had in his hands the possibility for two serious plays. He might write the story of a good young man with a tainted heritage, or he might describe the deleterious effect of metropolitan life on the individual. Instead he preferred to write a sensation drama, leaving the first possibility to Harley Granville-Barker *(The Voysey Inheritance)*, and the second to such later American playwrights as Elmer Rice and Clifford Odets.

The theatrical skill of Fitch and Belasco enabled them to invest their plays with a mask of urgency, convincing enough in the theater, but obviously to be replaced in its box when the play is ended. That the situations which they were exploiting for sentimental, melodramatic, or farcical purposes might be susceptible of close examination in terms of actuality did not concern them. Edward Sheldon, on the other hand centered many of his plots on such conflicts or problems as political corruption and the relationship between negroes and whites, of real concern outside the theater. He was bold in developing a vigorous action with unambiguous conflicts. If his work as a whole must be classed as theatrical rather than dramatic it is be-

cause his themes—the basic ideas which the actions support—are unreal or sentimental. The conclusions of his
plays are based on timeworn theatrical clichés rather than
on original analysis of the situation at hand.

The Nigger, produced at the New Theater in 1904, declares in its very title the immediacy of its subject. The
central figure, Philip Morrow, is a fine Southern gentleman who, while attempting because of his belief in rule by
law to save a young negro from lynching, nonetheless declares his position firmly in Act I:

> Things have changed some since the wah, an' if we want t'
> keep our blood clean, we've got to know that *white's white*
> and *black's black*—an' mixin' 'em's damnation.

On such a sentiment, Philip is elected governor of his state
and wins the hand of a charming belle, Georgie. Before
they can wed, however, Philip's old rival, Noyes, a whiskey
distiller, uncovers a long-hidden document, proving beyond
question that Philip's grandmother was a quadroon slave.
Noyes does not reveal his information until Philip is faced
with the alternative of signing or vetoing a prohibition
bill passed by the state legislature to better the lot of the
negro. The chief interest of the play thus becomes the questions which the hero must answer: Shall he compromise
with Noyes and thus save his love and his political future?
Shall he fearlessly face the fact and lose his sweetheart and
his position? Being a true Southern gentleman, or perhaps
being a typical hero, Philip faces the fact, and does the
honorable thing: he signs the bill and gives up Georgie.

There is a little more to *The Nigger* than the decision
itself. Philip is not allowed to get off easily; the letter is
no forgery and Noyes will certainly give it wide publicity.

And Georgie, after a momentary revulsion, comes tearfully back to Philip to announce that she still loves him and that they must go North together where marriage will be possible. Philip must therefore make a second decision, and he decides as his belief, stated in Act I, dictates. He must stay where he is and work for "his people," and Georgie will have to grin and bear it. He sympathizes with her position. "Yo's is the ha'dest fate," he says. "I've got wo'k ahead of me—lots of it, thank God! But you must sit with yo' han's folded—mo' or less—an' that's why I'm so . . ." Whereupon Georgie flings her arms about him and declares that she cannot give him up. "I'm jus' an o'dinary girl and I love you and I've got t' have you!" But Philip holds out, except to admit that he'll always love her, "till the very end." This, for some reason, satisfies the o'dinary girl: "I don't unde'stand, Phil *(With complete confidence)*. But somehow you've made me feel I'm wrong—an' that it's all right."

The serious, timely issues with which Sheldon began so boldly, have in this last act been smothered by a hackneyed working out of a lover's tragedy. Philip's sense of honor looks very much like blindness, and the lively Georgie of the earlier acts is replaced by the stereotyped helpless female cut from a second-rate lithograph. The none-too-honest situation is further falsified by its conclusion. When Georgie is leaving, Philip stops her for a moment:

Smile, Georgie, I want t' see you smilin'—! *(As she smiles bravely back at him)* Theah! That's the ticket! Keep it up, honey, an' remembah—it's all right—it's all right—it's comin' out all right.

Having filled his sweetheart (and his audience) with groundless optimism, Philip steps out on the balcony of the governor's mansion to reveal to the assembled citizens the story of his birth. But before he can speak, and before we can hear the public's reaction, the curtain falls as a band off-stage plays "America."

As the conclusion reveals, the theme of *The Nigger,* the idea that underlies the total action, is the power of romantic love. It is not, therefore, very far from *Madame Butterfly* as an instance of theatricalism, even making the mainspring of the plot the fortuitous discovery of a hidden letter. The long-lost letter is perhaps an economical way of motivating the action, but it is mechanical and inanimate. So the courageous attack on a very real problem in the first part of the play is turned into mere sensation or emotionalism at the end.

The same virtue, a subject drawn from matter of current interest, and the same defect, finding a solution to the problems raised in a too easy theatrical manipulation, are apparent in Sheldon's great success of 1911, *The Boss.* The play treats the conflict between social classes, a subject of universal concern, in the concrete terms of the efforts of an unscrupulous Irish boss to establish himself in the good society of his community. Ragan, the boss, is a well drawn and complex character, until the playwright's unerring sense of stage effect reduces him to pasteboard.

The basic conflict, between the established family and the interloper, between honest, unimaginative business management and impersonal ruthlessness, was particularly representative of the time. The Griswolds are the old family with a strong sense of personal honor and community responsibility, father and son operating a grain-transport firm and the daughter, Emily, earnestly working among the poor families of the dock hands. Ragan, by underpaying his men and keeping them drunk, is able to offer better rates than the Griswolds and gradually gets most of their contracts away from them. As the play begins, they are desperate over the imminent loss of their best customer to Ragan. This will not only mean bankruptcy for them but the failure of several banks whose money is invested in their firm. These banks, in turn, hold the small savings of those dock workers smart enough to be thrifty. Ragan, of course, offers a way out. If Emily Griswold will marry him, he will consent to a merger of the two firms and allow the Griswolds to run the new company according to their lights.

Emily sacrifices herself to a marriage in name only, and does her best to provide Ragan with the social contacts he yearns for. But her brother, Don, thinking of the family honor, resolves to break Ragan by organizing and leading a strike. Emily is now confronted with a new dilemma. Her brother tries to get her to disclose Ragan's scheme for defeating the workers, but she refuses because of her own sense of honor. When the Archbishop tries to reason her husband into compromising with the strikers and Ragan is provoked into attacking him, her sense of a higher honor goads her to reveal the secret plans for strikebreaking. As a result, the Archbishop addresses the strikers and strengthens their wavering determination. As the curtain falls on the second act, Ragan is vowing revenge on the Church, the Griswolds, and the community.

Unfortunately the real issue is befogged at intervals by Ragan's attempts to win the love of his wife. When she betrays him to the Archbishop he takes this as evidence of the hopelessness of his suit, and this, rather than the political or economic situation, really motivates his vengeance. With Cupid pulling the strings, Ragan, of course, is a lost man. Young Griswold is accidentally hit by a brick, flung by one of Ragan's henchmen, the town rises up in anger, and the Boss is arrested.

In the final act he is completely broken. In jail, his power gone, and, worst of all, unloved, Ragan gives up his revenge, takes on himself the guilt of another man, and generally comports himself in heroic fashion. The injured brother recovers, Emily learns of her husband's noble actions, discovers she loves him, and the play ends with the long-anticipated embrace. Superficially *The Boss* is about a social problem; actually love is the plot, love motivates and complicates the action, and the need for love in the foundation of a true marriage is the theme.

Sheldon's plays are startling proof of the determination of the theater of the early twentieth century to live in a world of its own. That he was not unaware of the world beyond the box office is apparent from his choice of settings and situations. But these settings and situations were selected only to give freshness and verisimilitude to conventional action and ideas. *The Nigger* and *The Boss* seemed startlingly real to contemporary audiences. The reality is only a device; it is not organic, it is not in the theme, the basic idea. The theme is as honest as the play is long.

2

TOWARD DRAMA

I<small>T IS</small> probably true that no play that survives its generation is altogether typical of that generation. Even the great theatrical successes considered above may be distinguished from the mass of lesser successes whose passing could not increase the vacancy of the vacuum they momentarily filled. But there is another group of plays of greater significance. These are not masterpieces; they are not compounded of those universals that make eventual revival inevitable. Doubtless they are forever condemned to historical anthologies, to be read and studied, but not produced save in the antiquarian spirit. Their distinction lies in the use which they make of the theatrical dexterity they share with the plays of Fitch and Sheldon and Belasco. They do not simply exploit the theater, they seem to be putting its skills and mechanics to further use.

An instance is to be found in William Vaughan Moody's *The Great Divide,* a play of adventure in the Western desert which was produced with great success in 1906. The year before, David Belasco had electrified his audiences with the stunning climax of his *Girl of the Golden West.* Belasco's hero, a wounded fugitive, has been hidden in a loft by "The Girl." She then attempts to convince the pursuing sheriff that his quarry is not there, finally engaging in a game of cards to demonstrate her nonchalance. The game is played in great detail, slow move after slow move, until, as the final play is reached and the sheriff is about to depart convinced, a drop of blood falls from the loft upon the card in his extended hand. This was the kind of sensation that Belasco and his audiences delighted in— an almost unendurable moment of suspense ended by an unforeseeable shock. No one would deny its effectiveness, or regret its employment. It is worth its weight in gilt.

Moody, a poet and professor as well as a playwright, was not at all ashamed to sit at the feet of the master. *The Great Divide* begins in a lonely prospector's cabin with the departure of all the occupants except a fearless young woman. As she prepares for bed, three men break in: Ghent, Dutch, and a Mexican. Sharing the same evil intentions, they fall to quarreling over who shall have possession of the woman. Ghent buys off the Mexican with a chain of nuggets; Dutch, however, will not yield his claim. The two agree to settle the matter by a shooting match, the loser to withdraw if physically able. At this point the men step outdoors and the terrified heroine is left alone in the cabin. We hear shots, and answering shots, and then—nothing. For a long moment the suspense is sustained. Finally the door opens, and Ghent reappears to claim his woman. This is a scene of theatrical effectiveness which Belasco might have envied, but he would have used it as his climax; for Moody it is the beginning of the drama.

Moody's conflict, that is to say, is more than simple good against simple bad with the ultimate triumph of the good. If good triumphs it is because the action of the play brings about an awakening of conscience, or consciousness, in his characters. Their increasing awareness of their situation is transferred to the audience, who recognize first the conflict between persons and later the more significant conflict between ways of life. The heroine represents the puritanical East, the hero the lawless West; through the action, the virtues as well as the defects of both ways of life are emphasized and a compromise achieved. The chorus character, Dr. Newbury, makes the author's point as he tries to reconcile the lovers. "Don't you think," he suggests, "that a mere difference of cultivation, polish—or—or something of that sort—is rather small to have led to a rupture, and so painful a one too?"

Moody, however, does not relax comfortably over this somewhat easy conclusion. In the tradition of the well-made play he makes great use of an inanimate object to advance his plot. In the first act Ghent "purchases" Ruth from the Mexican with a chain of unrefined gold. In the second act she has gone through the formality of a marriage while refusing him her love. By weaving blankets for tourists she gets enough money to buy the gold chain from the Mexican, wearing it as a reminder of her shame. At the end of the second act she flings it from her and departs for Massachusetts with her brother and sister-in-law. In her concentration on her own condition, however, she has not been aware of the change in her husband. She does not perceive that he has ceased to look upon her as a slave or squaw, as property, and has been trying to win her love as an individual. He recovers her chain, follows her to the East and, while keeping his distance, looks after her in secret. At the end, fully informed of his actions and understanding their meaning, Ruth takes the chain from him and puts it about her neck as a sign that she is no longer blind.

The chain thus becomes more than an inanimate object, a theatrical device; it acquires a thematic meaning. It is at first for both Ruth and Ghent the purchase money for a slave; but as the symbol of her shame it becomes for him an obstacle to their true union. His muddled efforts to understand the nature of his own actions lead to his development as a man, and these in turn lead Ruth to a perception of the true state of their relationship.

Moody, that is to say, is treating a subject of universal significance, the conflict between fundamental concepts of the good life. But these concepts are not simple, the virtues of each way are given fair statement, and the conclusion is sought in the modifications and compromises to which the action drives the characters. Ghent, not realizing that Ruth has shut her heart against him from the first, can say, just before the denouement: "You've fought hard for me, God bless you for it.—But it's been a losing game with you from the first!—You belong here in Massachusetts, and I belong out yonder—beyond the Rockies, beyond—the Great Divide!" The Great Divide is not simply the mountain range that stands between East and West, it is not merely the barrier between the civilized attitude towards woman and the more primitive. It is not so much a Continental Divide as a conventional divide, it is not between man and woman, but between ways of life.

The Great Divide has in it the stuff of great drama and of good theater. If it falls short of the highest level, it is

...aps because of a certain literary quality in the dialogue
...d the conventionality of its resolution. The personality
of the author frequently obtrudes upon the situation, as
when Ruth's sister-in-law, Polly, a not particularly literate
person, describes the heroine as "one of those people who
can't live in a state of divided feeling. She sits staring at
the cleavage in her life, like—like that man in Dante, don't
you know, who is pierced by the serpent, and who stands
there in hell staring at his wound, yawning like a sleepy
man." Yet for the average spectator, if not for the critical
student, it must have seemed that the resolution depended
not so much on an intellectual awareness of the situation
as upon the power of love to conquer all obstacles, however
mountainous.

At any rate, the comparative failure of Moody's last play,
The Faith Healer (1909), may have been due to his attempt to find a substitute for romantic love as a catalyst
in his action. Here he tells the story of Michaelis, a mysterious figure from the Far West, who comes to a Middle
Western community convinced that God has given him
the power to heal by faith. After an initial success, he is
diverted from his divine mission by the temptations of this
world, embodied in a young woman of no remarkable virtue. As a result he loses his power, but the young woman
has been moved by his effect on her relatives and neighbors. The faith which is born in her reawakens his own
faith and he is able to proceed upon his mission. And the
final moments of the play are devoted, not to the love that
provided a honeyed ending to all problems, but to the
power which delivers "all prisoned souls."

Moody displays the same technical skill as in his earlier
play. The opening situation is somewhat quieter, but the
conflict is no less strongly marked. Against Michaelis, as

the exponent of the power of the spirit, Moody sets Mr. Beeler, half-ignorant apostle of the "new" scientific spirit, a young doctor whose reaction to every event is cynical, and an old parson who is narrow and intolerant both of the advances of science and unorthodox manifestations of religious truth. Possibly the device whereby Michaelis falls in love with Rhoda, the cast-off mistress of the cynical doctor, makes too economical use of the theater; indeed, Dr. Littlefield seems to bring out the worst in the playwright (a not uncommon event in the portrayal of villains generally). Meeting Rhoda after a long separation he asks: "What in the world have you been doing all this time?"

RHODA: I have been searching for something.
LITTLEFIELD: What was it?
RHODA: My own lost self. My own—lost self.

This and Rhoda's subsequent speeches fail to be expressive of her character; they are over-ornate for the simple girl she is represented to be. So, when Michaelis is suddenly confronted with the fact that the girl he loves has been Littlefield's mistress, he resorts to the clichés of melodrama:

She gave you her young love, in childish blindness, not knowing what she did, and you killed it idly, wantonly, as a beast tortures its frail victim for sport. . . . Take your words and your looks from her, and that instantly, or you will curse the day you ever brought your evil presence into her life. (He advances upon him threateningly) Instantly, I say, or by the wrath of God your wretched soul, if you have one, shall go this hour to its account!

Such failures in expression are infrequent in the play, and are the more noticeable because of Moody's general success in keeping within the middle-class milieu he has set for his action. Although he invites incredulity by staging a miracle in a commonplace household inhabited by unexceptional characters, as a poet Moody is able to lend significance to the simple materials he permits himself. The action of the play, for instance, takes place during the Easter season. It is pointed out at the beginning of Act I that the weather is foggy and cold; in the midst of the act, Mrs. Beeler, the first patient, has a vision of the sun shining. So in Act III the victory of physical love over spiritual consecration is symbolized by a bright spring day—but this is no irony, for Michaelis' love awakens faith in Rhoda, which in turn results in the restoration of his own faith.

The smallest objects acquire symbolic meaning. Beeler makes much of his collection of scientific books and of a reproduction of the mocking picture, "Pan and the Pilgrim." At the moment of his wife's cure, he gets rid of them; at the moment of her relapse he refastens the picture to the wall. The meaning of the picture has been made clear not only by its obvious subject, but by a rambling story of a vision of the devil recounted by an old servant, which parallels Michaelis' account of his vision of Christ. Thus the placing and removing of the picture is not merely a typical, or spiteful, gesture of Beeler's, but an indication of the state of the moral conflict in the play. Mrs. Beeler makes the conflict explicit as she says of Michaelis:

Rhoda, I have seen him look at you so strangely! Like—like the Pilgrim in the picture, when he hears that heathen creature playing on the pipe.—You are such a wild creature, or you used to be.

So the two visions, of Christ and "the wine of this world," unite within Michaelis and very nearly result in his destruction as a man. But Rhoda's conviction restores his confidence, and the play ends on a note of religious ecstasy, the author rising above the simple realism of settings and characters by his lyric tone and expression. It fails as drama only when the cynic intrudes theatrically, a failure which is in a sense as symbolic of the meaning of the play as anything intended by the author.

The setting of *The Great Divide* is, of course, remote and romantic; the setting of *The Faith Healer* is within the experience of most members of the audience, the cluttered living room of a farmhouse. Such a setting requires from the playwright much closer attention to the naturalness of his characters and their speech. On the whole, Moody is successful in escaping from the clichés of his theater, the more notably because he has chosen a conflict which lends itself to rant and ornamental piousness. Falseness of diction is one of the major blemishes of plays of this period: characters speak in stagese, a language of their own, with an affected vocabulary and unnatural syntax which only emphasizes the artificiality of the play's action. If the playwright had 20/20 vision and a good ear for human speech, convention denied him their use. Belasco, Fitch, Sheldon, all are victims, perhaps unconsciously, of this convention. Moody, to a certain extent, escapes. And it is for his outright rejection of this convention that Eugene Walter deserves acknowledgment.

The Easiest Way (1909), Walter's greatest success, was intended to be a frankly realistic picture of a woman whose moral sense was considerably weaker than the other five. Laura Murdock, a minor actress and the mistress of Will Brockton, spends a summer in the Rockies, where she falls in love with John Madison, a vagabond. Love reforms them both; she plans to return to New York and earn her own living while he stays in the West prospecting to raise enough money to provide for their marriage. Brockton and Madison, who understand each other and their relationship to Laura, make a bargain—Brockton will leave her strictly alone, but should she slip back, he will inform Madison at once. Each man is confident of success, of his own analysis of the heroine's character. After some months in New York, Laura finds that it is nearly impossible to earn her living as an actress. Brockton has kept to the letter of his agreement by not attempting to influence her in person, but as a wealthy investor he has also been able to keep her out of the theater. (The theater, incidentally, is presented as a den of iniquity in accordance with the widely accepted American myth.) Out of work, about to be evicted for nonpayment of rent, hungry, Laura protests, "I know I could get jobs all right if I wanted to pay the price, but I won't."

Circumstances are finally too much for her and she goes back to Brockton. Mindful of his promise, and triumphant in his success, he forces her to write a letter to Madison explaining the situation, but she cannot bring herself to burn her bridges, and burns the letter instead. Madison, unaware of the change in her living arrangements, arrives from the West where he has made a rich strike in a gold field and begins making plans for their immediate marriage. When Brockton threatens to reveal the truth to him, Laura finally asserts herself, and in a rage drives her keeper from the apartment. The way is clear for a happy ending— but this is the theater, and 1909, and Madison finds out that Laura has lied to him and abandons her forever as the curtain falls.

The chief defect of *The Easiest Way* is the dishonesty of the action. None of the characters is a model of virtue, Madison least of all, yet they do not hesitate to pass judgments of almost puritanical strictness. Madison, in fact, is

a moral prig who refuses for one moment to consider the
real situation of the woman he supposedly loves. Laura
never has a chance, either to assert herself as an individual
or to present her case for impartial judgment. She is simply
treated as another member of the class established for the
theater by Dumas *fils* in *Le Demi-Monde* and exploited in
the English drama by Jones and Pinero, the fallen woman
who cannot be redeemed. Considered from the analysis of
its action, *The Easiest Way* is an addition to the repertory
of "Pinerotica": a somewhat risqué situation is resolved in
an eruption of conventional morality. As in the contemporary film, Laura is never permitted a moment of pleasure
in her sin and in the end the judgment on her is firm and, in
a double sense, manly.

On the surface, however, Walter is able to maintain a
convincing appearance of reality. There had been a few
efforts in the past, by such men as James A. Herne and
Denman Thompson, to reproduce on the stage the details
of American life. Thompson, in *The Old Homestead*
(1886), was defeated by his instinct for the sentimental so
that his sketches of life on the farm are little better than
calendar art. Though such plays as *Margaret Fleming* (1890)
and *Shore Acres* (1892) are faithful to life almost to the
last, real success eluded Herne because of his tendency to
overwrite the climactic scenes. Eugene Walter does not fall
victim of sentimentality, and he was apparently incapable
of any but the most commonplace language. As a result
the fundamental melodrama of the plot is considerably di-
luted by an appearance of mirroring life as its audience
could observe it. Walter can actually describe the play as
"more or less purely photographic," and Belasco, the producer, must have been delighted by the demands made
upon his ingenuity in reproducing natural effects by me-

chanical means. As the two men in the heroine's life discuss her and make their bargain, they are standing on an
outdoor terrace in the Rockies at sunset:

*As the Act progresses the shadows cross the Pass, and golden
light streams across the lower hills and tops the snow-clad
peaks. It becomes darker and darker, the lights fade to beautiful opalescent hues, until, when the curtain falls on the act,
with John and Will on the scene, it is pitch dark, with a faint
glow coming out of the door. Nothing else can be seen but
the glow of the ash on the end of each man's cigar as he puffs
it in silent meditation on their conversation.*

This "effect" might have been a step beyond the sensational Gas Chamber scene in *Sherlock Holmes,* but the step is
not taken. Walter and Belasco were content to use stage
mechanics to create mood, although the function of the
mood is somewhat obscure.

The extent to which author and producer were willing
to go to achieve a picture of life perfect in its details is apparent in the four pages devoted to describing the shabby
bedroom occupied by the heroine in her struggle to find
work in New York. After an extended description of the
room and its furnishings, the condition of the wallpaper
and the lighting fixture, and what can be seen from the
window, this paragraph follows:

*Under the mattress, at the head of the bed is a heavy cardboard
box, about thirty inches long, seven inches wide and four
inches deep, containing about a hundred and twenty-five letters and eighty telegrams, tied in about eight bundles with
dainty ribbon. One [bundle] must contain all practical letters
of several closely written pages each, each letter having been
opened. They must be written upon business paper and envelopes, such as are used in newspaper offices and by business
men.*

For all this apparent insistence upon the peculiarity or uniqueness of the individual letters, tied in eight bundles, and piled in a box of specified dimensions, they turn out to be the same overworked letters that had served to keep the plots of well-made plays in motion since the days of Eugène Scribe. *The Easiest Way,* considered as a whole, is not much more than an effective stage piece, but in the surface realism of its setting and the consistent underwriting of the dialogue it serves as a herald of the future.

Likewise prophetic was Langdon Mitchell's *The New York Idea* (1906) which remained unchallenged as high comedy until the plays of Philip Barry and S. N. Behrman began to appear in the twenties. The success of the play stems from Mitchell's apt combination of three elements, a central theme, a sense of structure, and a sense of humor. The theme, implicit in the title, is an examination of marriage, the "New York idea" being to take such a relationship lightly. As the English visitor declares:

New York is bounded on the North, South, East and West by the state of Divorce. . . . A 'thank you, ma'am.' That's what an American marriage is—a 'Thank you, ma'am.'[1] Bump—bump—You're over it and on to the next.

Mitchell is careful to stick to his theme, no extraneous matter or action is permitted to intrude.

The action is carefully arranged not only to yield the maximum amusement to the audience but to keep the audience constantly aware of the playwright's attitude towards his central idea. In Act I, Mitchell reveals the preparations for the marriage of Philip Phillmore and Cynthia Karslake. The chief comedy of the act derives from

[1] A once popular epithet for a bump in the roadway.

the introduction of their divorced wife and husband respec-
tively, and the kitty-corner sparring that ensues. This farce
is, however, given point by being set in a kind of scenic
parenthesis which opens and closes the act. In this scene
Cynthia's relatives-to-be discuss her and the marriage and
the proprieties until it is quite apparent that her "prudent"
marriage will be less happy than her unsuccessful "romantic" one.

In Act II, John Karslake defines Cynthia's trouble, why
their marriage could not succeed:

Our girls are brought up to be ignorant of life—they're ignorant of life. Life is a joke, and marriage is a picnic, and man is
a shawl-strap. . . .

an attitude echoed by her husband-to-be:

Marry for whim! That's the New York idea of marriage. . . .
Marry for whim and leave the rest to the divorce court! Marry
for whim and leave the rest to the man.

The action then contrasts the behavior of the ex-Mrs. Phillmore, as she schemes and plots to trap a second husband,
with Cynthia's avowed purpose, "To marry a friend—to
marry on prudent, sensible grounds." The denouement
comes as Cynthia realizes prudence to be as false a ground
for marriage as romantic whim, and as the ex-Mrs. Phillmore, having snared an English lord with her wiles, is taken
off by her new husband to rural England where the idea
of marriage is a permanent relationship blessed with many
children. Cynthia returns to her first husband recognizing
that her love for him plus their mutual interests and tastes
are more important than the whims or differences of opinion that led to their earlier separation. "I tell you," says

John Karslake, "marriage is three parts love and seven parts forgiveness of sins." The action of the play is thus designed to support clearly and effectively the central idea.

Mitchell's sense of humor manifests itself in many ways, in the crisscrossings of ex-husband, ex-wife, husband-to-be, wife-to-be, and in the wit of the dialogue, and in the characterization, particularly in the family portrait of the Phillmores. Matthew Phillmore is a parson, a society parson, and his characterization is a satire both on the type and on the society which finds the type acceptable. Here he describes his sermon of Sunday last:

My text was from Paul—"it is better to marry than to burn." It was a strictly logical sermon. I argued—that, as the grass withereth, and the flower fadeth,—there is nothing final in Nature; not even Death! And, as there is nothing final in Nature, not even Death;—so then if Death is not final—why should marriage be final? *(Gently.)* And so the necessity of—eh—divorce! You see? It was an exquisite sermon! All New York was there! And all New York went away happy! Even the sinners—if there were any! I don't often meet sinners—do you?

The wit, however, is always under control, never permitted to degenerate into mere gag. Like the structure it is organic to the central idea which controls the whole work. As a result of this control, and of the completely functional nature of each element involved, *The New York Idea* is one of the few enduring plays of the early twentieth-century American theater.

The tendency of that theater, as has become evident, was towards increasing realism, even though it was largely a realism of the surface. Something of an anomaly is *The Scarecrow* (1910), the most successful of the plays of the indefatigable experimenter, Percy MacKaye. But it is also prophetic, looking forward not only to the whole tradition of experimental drama which would flourish after the first World War, but to the fruitful attempts of the folk playwrights to draw materials from American legend, history, and tradition.

MacKaye had inherited all of his father's knowledge of practical stage effect, but aimed to turn it to more serious purposes. *The Scarecrow* is his dramatization of a tale by Nathaniel Hawthorne of an abandoned woman's revenge on her cruel lover. Aided by the Devil, she animates a scarecrow and sets it to wooing the niece of her former sweetheart, now a respectable magistrate in Puritan New England. Inspired by his experience of human love, the scarecrow becomes a whole man for a day. Standing beside a magic mirror, which reveals the true nature of the person it reflects, he confesses to the girl and her fiancé that he is but a thing of husks and pumpkin.

RAVENSBANE. Mistress, this pipe is I. This intermittent smoke holds, in its nebula, Venus, Mars, the world. If I should break it—chaos and the dark! And this of me that now stands up will sink jumbled upon the floor—a scarecrow. See! I break it. (*He breaks the pipe . . .*) Oh, Rachel, could I have been a man—!

He falls before the mirror which reflects, not a scarecrow but a normal man.

RAVENSBANE. A man! (*He falls back into the arms of the two lovers*) Rachel!
RICHARD. (*Bending over him*) Dead!
RACHEL. (*With an exalted look*) But a man!

Although this is a highly imaginative fantasy, that it has a theme and a serious one is evident from the outcome of the whole action, as well as from the quoted concluding speeches. *The Scarecrow* is a kind of psalm of life, or, perhaps, considering its material, a kind of folk-song of life, attesting the wonder and the necessity for self-realization, even though death awaits inevitably.

The action is skillfully managed in terms of the theme. The Devil, whose attitude towards man is completely cynical, is allowed to comment on the nature of man as he constructs the scarecrow:

Gourd, carrot, turnip, beet:—the anatomy. . . . *O Johannes Baptista!* What wouldst thou have given for such a head! I helped Salome to cut his off, dame, and it looked not half so appetizing on her charger. Tut! Copernicus wore once such a pumpkin, but it is rotten. Look at his golden smile! Hail Phoebus Apollo! *(. . . he stuffs the framework with the gourds, corn, etc. . . . weaving the husks about the legs and arms)* Here goes for the digestion and inherited instincts! More corn, Goody. Now he'll fight for his own flesh and blood.

The action of the play permits us to observe this inhuman patchwork first given a black-magical kind of life, and then converted into a man by the power of true love, so that the conclusion among other things is an answer to the cynicism of the Devil.

MacKaye describes *The Scarecrow* as a "tragedy of the ludicrous," the aptness of which depends upon his success in creating sympathy for his fantastic central figure. The long stage life of the play is witness to its ability to invoke pity for the hopeless state of its protagonist and admiration for the dignity with which he faces the inevitable. The materials for tragedy are certainly here.

If the effect of the play falls something short of tragedy, undoubtedly the nature of the materials is largely responsible. They are too fanciful to make a good case for Mac-Kaye's theme, while avoiding the conscious whimsy of *Peter Pan, The Wizard of Oz,* and the art-ballet. MacKaye demonstrated that subjects were at hand in folk history and legend that could be converted into exciting drama without appealing to sentimentality or melodrama. A lesson of great profit to the playwrights of the next generation.

3

FROM ROMANCE TO REALITY

As ANALYSIS has shown, even the best of the serious plays written by Americans before the first World War are not more than superficially true to life as we understand it. Nevertheless, they were successful with audiences, which is to say that the plays are true to life as their contemporary audiences desired or believed it to be. For if it were possible to sum up in one word the national temper in the era that followed the Spanish-American war, that word might well be complacency. Americanism of the George M. Cohan school was riding high, wide, and—in spite of Teddy Roosevelt's famous phrase—noisily. This was God's country and physical disasters and economic failures affected her only momentarily; the rumors of wars and revolutions abroad scarcely reached her ears. The successful plays of the first decade and a half of the century reflect a certain self-satisfaction, and their happy endings are not so much theatrical convention as popular conviction: there were few problems incapable of solution in this oversize Eden. But even the most innocent eyes must recognize the snake in the garden if a sharp enough light is thrown upon it. A series of events originating far back in the nineteenth century had brought illumination to practitioners of other arts (like Crane, Norris, and Dreiser in the novel), and at last the theater, which would have preferred to remain wrapped in red plush and cradled in a stage box, could no longer pretend there was nothing there.

In the earliest years of the twentieth century, the arts of the theater were being exploited for their own sakes, or used simply to narrate an exotic or amusing action. A few playwrights, like Moody, manifested some sense of the drama as an art as well as a sense of the theater as a machine. Their works become more nearly organic units, in which the theatrical components (setting, actors, dialogue, situation, and symbols) are employed to elucidate a theme. They thus, somewhat tentatively, were allying themselves with the great dramatic movement which, beginning in the middle of the nineteenth century in Europe, had produced the works of Ibsen, Strindberg, Chekhov, Shaw, Granville-Barker, and Galsworthy. Some of these revolutionary continental and British plays had made their appearance in the New York theater—Shavian comedy had even been notably successful as an item in the repertory of Richard Mansfield, the American matinee idol—but their influence had been infinitesimal: the occasional appearance of a sociological problem (*The Nigger*), closer attention to the literary values of the dialogue (*The New York Idea*), a recognition of the symbolic value of inanimate objects (*The*

Great Divide), a gesture towards honesty in characterization *(The Easiest Way),* a resort to unconventional materials *(The Scarecrow).* But in each instance the American playwright could scarcely be said to have been "influenced" from without. He was too timid, too tentative.

But the "War to End War" finally accomplished the long-delayed maturing of the American theater, and not simply because artists and audiences could no longer shut their eyes to the nature of a world that had been thrust under their noses. Among other things, the war period permanently established the movies as a popular entertainment medium, and the movies drew off from the legitimate theater the great mass of seekers after pure entertainment and simple affirmation. The audience that remained was less receptive to the easy cliché and the conditioned response. If it did not demand to be shocked, it would not tolerate being bored by the expected. It was not ignorant of books, or history, or life, and it was eager to have the chaos it observed outside the theater interpreted and shaped into an understandable work of art. This function the playwright and the drama were ideally suited to perform.

The revolution is, to be sure, more apparent thirty years after the event. At the time the great success of such masterpieces of mediocrity as *Three Wise Fools* and *Abie's Irish Rose* and *The Bat* far overshadowed, in the box-office handicap, *Anna Christie* or *Miss Lulu Bett.* The change which today appears cataclysmic, to its own time seemed merely the sparks from some eccentric fireworks in various "arty," noncommercial theaters.

The first step in this revolution, as has been indicated in discussing the first group of plays, was simply in the direction of greater realism. Mechanical realism had long been a part of the theater, stemming perhaps from the sensation scenes of melodrama. It is hard to say why an audience should take especial pleasure in seeing the actuality of an urban street, or a railroad station, or a lumber mill reproduced by the canvas and lathe and scene paint of the stage, but on such settings much of the attraction of the "10-20-30" popular drama was based. In the "serious drama" David Belasco was only one of many to make a career and a reputation out of meticulous attention to exact reproduction of the commonplace. And in the beginning, at least, realism of setting was a major aspect of the newly matured American drama.

Eugene O'Neill is a case in point. Although his later career revealed that he had other and more important concerns, in his first successful play for the commercial theater he devises his setting with close attention to details. Here is a portion of the direction for Act II, scene 1, of *Beyond the Horizon* (1920):

The [farmhouse sitting] room [as seen in the preceding act] has changed, not so much in its outward appearance as in its general atmosphere. Little significant details give evidence of carelessness, of inefficiency, of an industry gone to seed. The chairs appear shabby from lack of paint; the table cover is spotted and askew; holes show in the curtains; a child's doll, with one arm gone, lies under the table; a hoe stands in a corner; a man's coat is flung on the couch in the rear; the desk is cluttered up with odds and ends; a number of books are piled carelessly on the sideboard. The noon enervation of the sultry, scorching day seems to have penetrated indoors, causing even inanimate objects to wear an aspect of despondent exhaustion.

It is interesting to compare the details of this setting with the details quoted from the setting of Act II of *The Easiest Way* (see p. 32). They are no less precise, but more organic. The details in the earlier play simply accommodated a sensational plot development; the details in *Beyond the Horizon* establish the place recognizably, but they symbolize the change which the action of the play has brought about in particular characters. Without for a moment transgressing the bounds of reality, or what the audience would recognize as reality, they are more than a device for enclosing the situation or advancing the plot. While they are related to the development of the action, the relationship is thematic, organic; they make explicit something about the inner conflict which is O'Neill's principal concern in the play.

Likewise, the setting demanded by Sidney Howard in *The Silver Cord* (1926) is at once symbolic and realistic:

A living room, built and decorated in the best manner of 1905, and cluttered with the souvenirs of maternal love, European travel, and an orthodox enthusiasm for the arts. There is a vast quantity of Braun Clement and the Arundel Society reproductions of the Renaissance Italian masters. The piano features Grieg, Sibelius and MacDowell. A door gives on a spacious hallway. Windows overlook a spacious garden.

At first glance the setting is a realistic reproduction of a middle-class parlor; looking more closely, the spectator observes that the details of the room have been selected to suggest the nature of the occupant or owner. This is not the mechanical realism of melodrama or Belasco; it is organically related to both the action and the basic idea of the play. It is a step beyond the surface truth of realism to the inward truth of selective realism.

The same advance may be noted in the characters selected by the playwrights. The popular drama had long abandoned the lords and ladies and the romantically recollected heroes and heroines of history and legend. Melodrama had been chiefly concerned with sailors and firemen and farmers and other members of the commonalty. Fitch and Moody and Walter had confined themselves democratically to the middle class. But the characters of melodrama invariably, and those of Fitch and Walter generally, were stereotypes whose reality was of the surface, a matter of make-up rather than inner truth. If theatergoers looked back with fondness on Fitch's *Captain Jinks of the Horse Marines* (1901), it was to recall Ethel Barrymore's playing of the leading role; but the most devoted fan would be hard put to remember the name and nature of her character.

After 1915, however, the American drama is filled with characters memorable in themselves, characters who have survived the actors who first impersonated them. The actual name of the title character in George Kelly's *The Show-Off* may slip the mind, but the character himself remains a vivid, living image. The sailors of O'Neill's Provincetown plays of the sea are drawn from his own observation and understanding of such men, and not from a gallery of theatrical types. They are born of the necessity of the situation, not of the theatrical demand that favorite actors be provided with opportunities to display themselves in favorite roles. It is both simple and instructive to compare the dirty, profane, cynical army men of *What Price Glory?* with the dapper, romantic, idealistic military heroes of Bronson Howard's *Shenandoah* (1888), or O'Neill's fallen woman in *Anna Christie* with Walter's heroine in *The Easiest Way*. In the more mature dramas the characters are conceived as a part of their environment, shaped and conditioned by their past experiences, and reacting to the situations that confront them in their own way, not the way of theatrical tradition.

It becomes increasingly difficult to classify the characters as villains and heroes. The firm morality (of the theater) prevented the heroine of *The Easiest Way* from claiming our sympathy; Anna Christie's lot is much the same, but because she is portrayed honestly she arouses pity and demands understanding.

Equally clear is what might be called the increasing realism of situation. The older theater demanded "strong" situations: true love growing out of near-rape, the discovery of negro blood in an advocate of white supremacy. Some of the new playwrights, notably O'Neill, did not abandon such violent or shocking turns of fate; but many were content with domestic conflicts, with the problems of adolescence, with the morality of a society adrift. It must not be supposed that the abandonment of strong situations diminished the excitement of playgoing. The purpose of the new playwright was to draw the spectator into the action personally and completely. He no longer observed with interest conflicts involving persons whom he could see, as it were, only from a distance. These plays presented his people and his problems and conflicts, and he had a personal stake in the working out of the situation. The plays of George Kelly are particularly strong instances of this principle, but Sidney Howard's exposure of "momism" in *The Silver Cord,* or Zona Gale's picture of the good-hearted family drudge in *Miss Lulu Bett* make equally effective use of everyday experience.

Realism of character and situation are a prelude to realism of action. No longer could the audience be certain that an overdue letter or an unexpected legacy would arrive in the last act to set everything to rights and bring about a happy ending. Of love stories in particular the older playgoers might complain with the character in *Love's Labour's Lost:*

> Our wooing doth not end like an old play:
> Jack hath not Jill.

In *Craig's Wife,* the nature of the heroine leads to the collapse of her marriage; *Lucky Sam McCarver* demonstrates that love and marriage do not inevitably lead to reformation or compromise; even *Anna Christie,* which seems to deal with the salvation of a prostitute, ends ambiguously: the characters of the play have reached only a resting place, the falling curtain does not make an end of their story. The inner nature of Anna and Chris and Matt will not allow them to remain settled for long, and fate or necessity or "dat ole davil sea" will drive them on to further torment and unhappiness.

But the most important element in the new drama was a realism of theme. Earlier playwrights were continually thwarted by the requirement of fitting their action to some moralistic truism that had little relation to the facts of life as experienced by themselves or their audiences. Their plays were designed to demonstrate that love is a wonderful thing, that kind hearts are more than coronets, that there is no redemption for fallen women, that one American is worth four of the citizens of any other nation. The themes of the new realism, on the other hand, are the immediate concerns of the audience, and their selection indicates the theater's growing seriousness of purpose and the playwright's growing awareness of his responsibility. No longer is his view of life bounded by the rising and falling of a velvet curtain. The crumbling of beliefs, the withering of conventions, and the ideological and political conflicts have become savage and inescapable.

The playwright's reaction was to roll up his sleeves and go into the market place. With intense conviction he pulled down the revered stereotypes which had been his dependable guides: the inviolability of marriage, the sanctity of mother love, the heroism of war, the respectability of commerce.

Realism, of course, has its limitations. Frequently the subject matter of these plays is journalistic as in *Broadway* (1926), *The Racket* (1927), or *Five Star Final* (1930); the passing of prohibition and yellow journalism, or the achievement of municipal reforms, left them little better than historical curiosities. Even plays like *Lucky Sam McCarver* which are principally concerned with fundamental human relations acquire a patina of the antique because they are founded on conditions which no longer exist. Those plays of the new realism which have lost little of their original vitality generally restrict themselves to the minute observation of men in the ordinary and eternal conflicts of everyday living, or by the use of symbols escape over the boundaries of realism into the evergreen and limitless fields of poetic truth.

It is not difficult to find evidence of the limitations of realism. There is for instance a group of plays from the late twenties which might be described as mirrors of the metropolis. Their manner is journalistic and their purpose to exploit the setting. The Big City is not the background for the action, it is the reason for the action. Reference has already been made to *Broadway, The Racket,* and *Five Star Final.* To these might be added *The Front Page* (1928), in which Ben Hecht and Charles MacArthur pretend to satirize but actually idolize the callous antics of reporters for the sensational press, and *The Barker* (1927) and *Burlesque* (1927), slightly sentimentalized documents describing the seamier aspects of the theater. Effective as these plays were in their own day, passing years and changing conditions have sapped their vitality. They are not, indeed, far from that melodrama that existed to exploit the wonders of the steam locomotive, the wireless telegraph, and the fire engine, or to explore the secret vices of the Bowery, Chinatown, or the Parisian *demi-monde*.

Although Sidney Howard, in *Lucky Sam McCarver* (1925), is concerned with the larger problems of marriage and human relationships, his success in creating a realistic background for his action to some extent destroys the focus of his play. If his hero, Sam McCarver, is a universal type, his heroine, Carlotta, is very much the product of her time and her milieu. The details of the business management of a speakeasy still have a certain amount of interest, but the picture of the footling life of the rich expatriates in Italy is so fantastic that only an intimate acquaintance with the period could lead to its acceptance as real. Yet Howard depends upon the reality of his background to lend conviction to the behavior of his characters. He calls the play "Four Episodes in the Rise of a New Yorker," and declares his purpose to have been,

to represent the two most spectacular extremes of the American social pendulum as it swings, in all its shoddiness of standards and philosophy, across the handsome horizon [of New York life].

Sam is ruthless, self-made, calculating, the proprietor of a speak-easy; Carlotta is rich, high in society, pleasure-mad, world-weary, and thoughtless. Theirs is not a loveless marriage, but love is unable to overcome the dominant forces in their personalities. However much he may love Carlotta, Sam is using her for his own advancement; however much she may love Sam, Carlotta must follow her whim. The result is a rather sensational death scene, as Carlotta dies repentant while Sam, who is now advancing towards other goals, seems to wonder what all the fuss is about. If Howard is true to his realistic purpose in refusing to contrive a happy ending, the death scene is nonetheless on the melodramatic side, with the two leading characters brought together, quite unnaturally, for the sake of a big moment—signifying not much. For Howard is never clear about what makes these people behave as they do: is it inner necessity? fate? environment? Or is it, as in the last scene, the will of the dramatist? The play fails as realistic drama because it does not penetrate to the deepest reality, because it fails somehow to tell the whole truth.

Although George Kelly is among the most successful of the realists (see p. 121) his *Behold the Bridegroom* (1927) is curiously unsatisfactory. The play is a character analysis of a woman somewhat like the heroine of *Lucky Sam McCarver*. Tony Lyle is a bored, restless member of the upper class living dangerously, a thoroughly bad girl. Totally preoccupied with herself and her own pleasure, she has taken especial delight in flirting with married men, breaking up homes, and generally in behaving with complete moral irresponsibility. She is only bewildered by the action of her friend, Mrs. Ridgway, who gave up riches for a penniless young man, declaring that she has found excitement and real interest in life in working him up to success. Then Mrs. Ridgway introduces Tony to a man not from her own class. Almost automatically she makes a play for him, but unlike Sam McCarver he does not respond. He understands her and "holds her cheap." From his unwillingness to have anything to do with her, she comes to recognize herself as one of "those caricatures of women. . . . Disillusioned and divorced, and married and divorced again." Following the pattern set by Carlotta McCarver, she loses her will to live, sickens and dies.

Sidney Howard believed that love was not strong enough to overcome other elements of human nature; Mr. Kelly apparently proposes the opposite opinion. Tony's inability to capture the man she really loves leads her for the first time to an awareness of herself, an understanding of her situation. This is a legitimate and frequently employed subject for tragedy, yet *Behold the Bridegroom* falls considerably short of its goal. Tony is presented and analyzed in detail; everything about her is convincing, even her change of purpose, if "love conquers self-love," is an acceptable precept.

Unfortunately, Tony's young man, Spencer Train, is something less than impressive. At the end of the play his behavior is so ambiguous that he hardly seems worth dying for. Mr. Kelly has seen fit to make considerable use of a rather elementary symbol throughout the play. The setting is Tony's room which overlooks a rose garden apparently barren of blossoms. When the young man enters he is carrying a white rose, the only flower in the garden: "Behold the bridegroom cometh." After he has left, Tony keeps the rose pressed in the pages of a book. This volume Spencer opens after the announcement of her death.

TRAIN. She said she wasn't *ready* when the *bridegroom* came. . . . I'm wondering if *I* was ready, Eleanor.

MRS. RIDGWAY. But you *were* the bridegroom, Spencer—

TRAIN. No, I think perhaps the bridegroom, Eleanor, is the kind of thing that she had to give; and I think, if I'd been ready, I might have recognized it sooner than I did:—And it might not *come* my way again.

[*He looks at the rose, then reverently places it in the book.*]

Such an ending reverts to the worst conventions of romantic opera and domestic melodrama. By rights it should be followed by a tenor aria, or an announcement from the stage manager that next week's play will be *East Lynne*. Had Mr. Kelly stood honestly by his character and not forced him to degenerate into the sentimentality of a maudlin symbol, the play would certainly have been stronger. Here at least Howard's work is more successful: Sam McCarver is himself at the end as at the beginning of his play. And relating the failure of *Behold the Bridegroom* to Kelly's success in general, it can only be concluded that he had trespassed upon an environment he did not understand. The complete verisimilitude of successful realistic drama demands not only accurate observation by the playwright but a penetration by his heart and mind beneath the surface apparent to all other beholders.

Meticulous surface realism is characteristic of the plays of Sidney Kingsley. In *Dead End* (1935) he reproduced upon the stage a slum area complete with a dock from which a large cast of juvenile delinquents dived into the orchestra pit, to appear moments later, glistening wet. The delight which the audience took in such effects and their curiosity about how they were achieved, of course, destroyed much of the dramatic illusion. *Men in White* (1933) is remembered largely because of the minute reproduction of the procedures in the operating room of a hospital, a scene which throws the action of the play off-balance and has almost no relation to the play's theme. More recently, in *Detective Story* (1949), Kingsley seems to have begun with a theme (it is the theme of *Measure for Measure*) which the main action of the play clearly supports. However, he has chosen a district police station as his setting, and he has so filled it with minor criminals and justice-seeking citizens that the focus frequently wavers from the main concern of the play. Like his earlier works, *Detective Story* may be said to suffer from small literalness. Kingsley's realism frequently results in a clutter.

The obverse of this is the major defect of Arthur Miller's *All My Sons* (1947). Miller takes great pains to reproduce a setting which will instantly strike his audience as natural, as normal. It is the backyard of an American home, with the rear of the house occupying most of the upstage area. Miller describes the poplar trees which mark the boundary of the property, the driveway, a small summerhouse, garden chairs and tables. Every detail is there, even the garbage pail and incinerator. But the characters of the play and the situations are, if the word is allowable, over-selected. There is a kind of deliberateness in the arrangement of the details of the action which makes the spectator aware of the mechanics of the playwright's art. Miller is directing all his efforts to one end, the elucidation of his theme, and there is not a superfluous character or action. Few plays for the contemporary theater have been planned with such care and skill. If *All My Sons* lacks conviction today, it is because the timeworn machinery of suppressed information takes too important a place in the denouement.

The hero, Joe Keller, accused of selling defective airplane motors to the government, manages to throw the blame on his partner, and squares his conscience by declaring that his whole thought was for his family which would naturally have suffered from the loss of revenue if the parts had not been sold. In the last ten minutes of the play the heroine, fiancée of Keller's son, reads a letter which she has been carrying about for three acts, revealing that he has heard of his father's actions, and knows the number of fliers who died as a consequence; and that he himself will not return from the mission on which he is about to start. The action, like the setting, concentrates on the central idea, made overt in the words of Keller's surviving son, who says to his father, "Once and for all, you can know that the whole earth comes in through those fences; there's a universe outside and you're responsible to it, and if you're not, you threw your son away, because that's why he died." In recognition and expiation, Keller kills himself.

All My Sons is thus almost a classic example of the well-made, realistic play with a thesis. Because of the emotional appeal of the thesis, the contemporary audience was blinded to the contrivances by which the point was made. Any play, even the most realistic, must of course be contrived. But the nature of the playwright's devices is important; he cannot be equally realistic and artificial. One or the other quality must be subordinated if the work is to carry conviction.

Those plays of the new realism which have lost little of their original vitality generally restrict themselves to the minute observation of man in the ordinary and eternal conflicts of daily life. Many of these plays concern themselves with middle-class life in the suburbs along the East Coast or in the cities of the Midwest. Upper-class life remains a subject for comedy of manners or farce, and the lower classes were—at first—left alone. Time enough for them when the new realists had exhausted the possibilities of small businessmen and their families.

The new realism achieved recognition when *Miss Lulu Bett,* dramatized by Zona Gale from her own novel, was awarded the Pulitzer Prize for the 1920-21 season. Actually Miss Gale is retelling the fairy tale of Cinderella, the family drudge who is liberated by Prince Charming and rewarded with all desirable things, but the realistic intention has led to some significant deviations from the classic pattern. Lulu, who lives with her sister and brother-in-law, earns her keep by doing the housework and looking after her mother and her young nieces. Contrary to expectation, she accepts her position, understanding its menial nature while reserving the right to exercise a reasonably sharp tongue. Contrary to expectation, the shrewish, grumbling old mother is permitted in the end to act generously towards her unlikely daughter and to defy her shallow, domineering son-in-law. Contrary to expectation, the youngest daughter is anything but a curly-headed toddler; she is thoroughly unpleasant, spoiled, and not the least attractive. Prince Charming, something less than dashing, is a commonplace, unromantic man, and Lulu herself, even when she finds love and happiness in marriage, is never transformed into a princess.

Although realism in setting was more to be expected, Miss Gale has an eye for the significant detail. The dining room of the first act, with its *Plain rose paper. . . . Large pictures of, say, "Paul and Virginia" and Abbott Thayer's "Motherhood,"* or the side porch of the second act with its wicker furniture and missing screens tell the audience more directly, more economically than all the naturalistic clutter of "Belascoism" what sort of a family they had to deal with.

Of greater importance is the realism of the dialogue, for it is here that most playwrights fall short of their intentions. A character in a play would be intolerably dull if he were permitted to speak diffusely, without focus or selection, as in everyday conversation. On the other hand, he becomes incredible if his speech is overcontrolled, over-"dramatic." Miss Gale has an ear, not merely for the vocabulary of the average man, but for the rhythms of his speech.

DWIGHT. Where's your mother? Isn't she coming to supper?
INA. No. Tantrum.
DWIGHT. Oh ho, mama has a tantrum, eh? My dear Ina, your
mother is getting old. She don't have as many clear-headed
days as she did.
INA. Mama's mind is just as good as it ever was, sometimes.

The delicately misplaced adverb in Ina's last speech is
doubly effective: it is a kind of comic afterthought, and it
conveys the impression of the aimless phrasing of common
talk. And a moment of introspection, of character revelation, gains conviction from the simplicity of expression.
Mrs. Bett is explaining why she has never allowed Lulu to
marry:

NINIAN. Don't you think she'd be better off?
MRS. BETT. Wouldn't make much difference. Why, look at
me. A husband, six children, four of 'em under the sod with
him. And sometimes I feel as though nothin' more had happened to me than has happened to Lulie. It's all gone. For
me just the same as for her. Only she ain't had the pain. (Yawns)
What was I talkin' about just then?

Miss Lulu Bett is a simple play, attempting to convey
its interpretation of life in the direct terms of simple realism: everyday speech, everyday characters, and everyday
locale. In the final evaluation, however, it is important to
observe to what use these elements have been put, what
function the play as a whole serves. Towards the end of
the third act, Lulu turns on her brother-in-law who has
been taunting her, and says, "You've pretended so long you
can't be honest with yourself, any of the time. Your whole
life is a lie." The action of the play has drawn an explicit
picture of Dwight, of his shabby ideals, his pretentious
speech, his self-confident behavior. He is not, in the lan-

guage of the play's background, "genuine." Lulu, on her side, is completely true, to herself, to the man she marries, to her responsibilities. In a larger sense, she represents the playwright who is "true" in the same ways to her characters, to her action, to her responsibilities as an artist. Here the deviations from the conventional treatment of Cinderella become important; they are on the side of truth. Thematically the play is an attack on small-minded hypocrisy; dramatically it demonstrates the virtues of truthful reproduction of honest observation.

In view of the general honesty of the play it is disappointing to discover that much of the suspense in the second act depends upon the contents of a letter which lies, tantalizing and unopened, in full view of the audience. If this relapse into theatricalism is surprising in Miss Gale, it is to be expected in the works of the older hands, playwrights who had earned their living if not their laurels by furnishing the popular theater with pasteboard sensations. Of these none was more firmly established or rigidly classified as a popular hack than Owen Davis, who had since the early years of the century produced a stream of farces and melodramas of the shoddiest sort. When he abandoned the easy trickery of the 10-20-30 to struggle with the new realism it seemed to the theater-wise that he was simply seizing some new decoration for his hackneyed, conventional plots, that the elements of "realism" would serve as novelties, as fresher substitutes for the overworked steam engines, fire apparatus, and sewing-machine girls.

Not that *The Detour* (1921) wholly escapes theatricalism. Its structure is too pat, and the working out of its plot too logical to be lifelike. In contrast with the deliberately underwritten curtain lines of *Miss Lulu Bett,* Mr. Davis cannot resist the temptation to signal for his intermissions with a ringing speech or a violent gesture. And possibly the insistence upon the reality of the faucet in the kitchen and the reality of the screen on the door is a kind of Belascoism.

Yet there is a seriousness about what happens in *The Detour* that was lacking in Mr. Davis' earlier plays. Not only do the characters for the most part determine the selection and development of situations, but they live by a simple understanding of life which audiences could not fail to recognize as their own. After a quarrel between husband and wife, the young hero remarks, somewhat obviously: "He's mad."

HELEN. He'll get over it!
TOM. *(Doubtfully)* I don't know!
HELEN. You've never been married. If you had you'd know there ain't anything else for married folks to do.

And when the young farmer explains to his girl why he cannot sympathize with her desire to be an artist:

I ain't an artist—artists like things that are pretty just because they are pretty—I don't care nothin' about 'em unless they're *mine!*

In suggesting this theme, Mr. Davis anticipates one of O'Neill's most powerful dramas, and it is perhaps significant that both share a New England background, inherited or acquired. But the theme is not developed. Instead *The Detour* abandons its realism in the last act for some highly effective stage comedy, and muddies its theme by a symbol which acquires meaning from an artificial coincidence. The problem of the play, once the limelight of theatricalism is turned upon it, cannot be taken too seriously.

Some estimation of the grip of realism on the American theater after World War I may be gained from the titles awarded the Pulitzer Prize as the best plays of their seasons. Between 1917 and 1927 there were ten awards; eight of these were for realistic plays.

Owen Davis received a Pulitzer prize for *Icebound,* a drama of village life in Maine. Produced in 1923, *Icebound* sticks more closely to its realistic guns than *The Detour;* there are no comic scenes to get in the way of the action, the dialogue is simple, effective, and not theatrical, nor are there too many obvious localisms. The situation is a trifle reminiscent of Pinero's *The Thunderbolt* as the rising curtain reveals the unattractive members of an ingrown family assembled to await the death of a matriarch. The action of the play deals with the regeneration of the family black sheep and the thwarting of the greed of the other relatives.

The action by itself is not particularly fresh or novel, redemption of the unredeemed by love being a standard subject for drama. But the characters, while they may be related to familiar types, have been observed from life. The happy ending is not unexpected, but it is accomplished without heroics or sentimentality.

Such plays as *Craig's Wife* (1925) and *The Silver Cord* (1926) achieve a fuller realism by penetrating beyond the surface of wallpaper and bird's-eye maple bedroom suites to the inward realities of the problems facing the contemporary audience. Both plays are character sketches of domineering females, both have implicit in them a plea for the rights of individuals. Howard shows in *The Silver Cord* how mother love can turn to egocentric tyranny; Kelly's title character in *Craig's Wife* is a woman whose sense of possession controls her life. At first it is simply her home and its furnishings that she possesses so fanatically. Later, she begins to absorb her husband. At this he revolts and leaves the house, abandoning his wife and most of his possessions. And Mrs. Craig is left alone with the material property she valued so highly.

The Silver Cord finds a happier though no less important solution. Here a mother, for her own selfish purpose, tries to keep her two grown sons tied to her apron strings. The wife of one of the boys manages to rescue her husband from the maternal trap just before it finally closes. After his fiancée has been driven to attempt suicide, the younger son is content to stay home with mother, receiving the protection and adulation she ladles out in generous portions as a recompense for destroying his life. The effectiveness of the play lies in this double ending, part happy, part pathetic. The older drama had of course presented domineering mothers, but, like shrewish wives, they were figures of fun and were generally defeated at the end. That Mrs. Phelps is half-victorious is a dramatically effective demonstration of the power which the playwright is attacking. Her complete defeat might have been more satisfying emotionally, but it would have been intellectually unconvincing.

The play, like those of Zona Gale and Owen Davis, suffers from "dramatic tact." This phrase was happily coined by a Victorian playwright to put the best face possible on his practice, and it means the employment of over-efficient, over-economical means of proving a dramatic point. The old reliable devices of suspense and preparation, from the conventions of the well-made play, are used to forward the plot. Analysis of the action, too, suggests that the elder son escapes from his mother not because he has really freed himself from her influence, but because he is more greatly dominated by another woman, his wife. However, the real-

ity of the theme and the basic situation, presented seriously
for the first time in the modern theater, compensates for
Mr. Howard's occasional lapse from the art into the craft
of playwrighting.

It is probably true that the realistic playwright with a
thesis, a message, is bound to appear more the artificer than
his simpler brother with nothing but a story to tell. Several
instances of this have already been adduced: of Owen
Davis' two plays, *Icebound* is constructed on a universal
theme and thus preserves its atmosphere of reality; *The
Detour* is constructed about a particular incident, an atypi-
cal relationship, and resorts to ingenuity to work out its
plot. In the hands of a highly accomplished craftsman, of
course, the mechanics are usually hidden from the spectator's eye, and this fact is sufficient to give the play vitality
and conviction for its immediate audience. Yet the careers
of two generally successful propaganda-playwrights, Lillian
Hellman and Clifford Odets, demonstrate that conviction
can sometimes overcome craftsmanship to the serious detri-
ment of even theatrical effectiveness.

In 1939, Miss Hellman's great success, *The Little Foxes,*
was the final proof of the theatrical skill suggested by such
a play as *The Children's Hour* (1934). The savage portrait
of a family of Southern millowners has not been equalled
on our stage for its effective combination of brutality and
pathos. Undoubtedly in the playwright's mind as the play
took shape was the underlying idea that the actions of the
Hubbards exemplified the inhumanity and vices of capitalism. Yet the impact on audiences was that of a much
more general theme: the senseless destruction of the good
by an almost motiveless evil. It was this theme rather than
the more specific one which made the play such a terrify-
ing experience to witness.

But in two plays written under the pressure of the second World War, *Watch on the Rhine* (1941) and *The Searching Wind* (1944), Miss Hellman was so caught up in contemporary issues that the structure of the drama in each case is faulty and the impact weakened. *The Little Foxes* was effective in part because of the humanity of its inhuman characters. That is, however wretchedly they behaved, their motives were clear and familiar; and the characters and their motives constituted the drama, rather than any commentary they were supposed to be making on our economic system. In the later plays Miss Hellman has divided her attention between human motives and political commentary. The love story in *Watch on the Rhine* which might have been poignant seems only an intrusion in an intrigue compounded of Nazi traitors and isolationism. *The Searching Wind* attempts to relate a love triangle to changes in American foreign policy. The resultant confusion dehumanizes the lovers and makes trivial the problems of international relations.

Clifford Odets, whose zeal for social reform has burned now bright now dim throughout his career, has never been as technically skillful as Miss Hellman, but in at least one element of the drama he has been unequalled in the modern theater: he has, or had, an absolute ear for human speech. Thin as his characters might be, or obscure, or conventional, and unconvincing the situations in which they were set adrift, they seldom failed to sound alive, to sound human and three-dimensional.

Odets' first full length play, *Awake and Sing!* (1935), is without question the most successful of the many treatments of bourgeois life against the narrow background of the Bronx, New York. Nothing could be more commonplace than the humble life of the Berger family; it is the story of what Mr. Roosevelt used to call "one-third of a nation." There are Old Jacob, the grandfather, thoroughly bewildered by his fate in what he had thought a land of promise, taking refuge in the philosophy and rhetoric of Marx and Engels; Myron, the father, the born follower, too weak to be dissatisfied with his own failure; Hennie and Ralph, the children, full of vague discontents, but prevented by their environment from taking positive action, or even seeing what positive action is possible. And there is Bessie, the mother, who holds the family together by her middle-class pride, her old-fashioned energy, competence, and shrewdness.

Some of the things that happen to the Bergers used to happen regularly in melodrama. Hennie is about to have an illegitimate child—but Myron is too weak to order her never to darken his door again, and Bessie sets about trapping an innocent young immigrant into marrying her. Also, close to the older convention, young Ralph gets his start finally when he inherits $3000 from grandfather Jacob. But it is important to notice the difference in just these two situations. Hennie is never punished for her "sin," but is made legally respectable. And Ralph gets his money because his grandfather recognizes in him both the opportunity for improvement which he himself could not seize and the drive for self-betterment which Myron lacked; Jacob commits suicide that Ralph may have his insurance. The play is a picture, a picture of life in a society in which life is printed on dollar bills, a bitter, honest, and living picture.

Awake and Sing! is an astonishing achievement for a first play, and one Odets has found it hard to equal. Yet it has its limitations. The motive behind the writing was propagandist, and the characters and situations are thus carefully selected to illustrate the theme. The result is a rather special picture of family life in the city, a kind of case history with a moral. It might be compared with two very different treatments of metropolitan life: with Clyde Fitch's *The City* which proposed to demonstrate the evil effect of urban life on a good family; with Elmer Rice's *Street Scene* (1929).

Rice presented his audience, not with a single family living under carefully controlled conditions, but with a cross section of city life as experienced by a large group of people who live in or are somehow connected with a huge brownstone tenement. They are varied in racial background, in philosophy, in occupation, in social status and intellectual stature: Italians, Jews, Swedes, Irish, musicians, electricians, milkmen, teachers, radicals, conservatives, poets and peasants. Yet the audience is not conscious that a cross section has been selected and presented to it; what is more natural in the melting pot of New York than that such a mixture occupy one tenement and animate one plot?

The plot, what there is of it, is hackneyed. *Street Scene* is really a conversation piece centering on a love triangle. But adultery and murder are not the exclusive interests of the play. More important is the play's attempt to present a generalized picture of middle-class urban living, an attempt so successful on the whole that the playwright was called a "mere journalist," and other terms suggesting critical disapproval.

Street Scene is anything but journalism. It is actually a kind of domestic symphony, taking the details of life, each as accurately rendered as possible, and arranging them within a frame (or perhaps better, against a background) that is itself a familiar commonplace, to yield an interpretation of what this crowded communal life means in terms of the individual and the group. Unlike *Awake and Sing!* the play seems to have no propagandistic purpose, unless it is expressed by Mrs. Maurant:

I often think it's a shame that people don't get along better, together. People ought to be able to live together in peace and quiet; without making each other miserable.

Feeble as the sentiment is, it is characteristic of the speaker and pertains to every situation in the play. *Street Scene* is selective realism at its best.

While selective realism defines Rice's play accurately, the term might be applied carelessly to such plays as *Lucky Sam McCarver* and *The Detour,* to which exception was taken on the grounds that over-manipulation of realistic details resulted in a loss of verisimilitude. Rice selects and arranges with the ultimate purpose of giving an impression of life, his predecessors with the purpose of exposing a defect or winning an argument. The poet and the district attorney may use the same facts to make a narrative and a case, but the one is aiming at the truth, the other at persuasion regardless of the truth. If selective realism is an acceptable term it is proper to restrict it to those plays in which the manipulation of observed fact results in the revelation of hidden or more general truths than accurate reproduction of the apparent reality could yield. Foremost of the selective realists, of course, is Eugene O'Neill, but the term also applies to Philip Barry (to his better half), and to such contemporary playwrights as Irwin Shaw and Arthur Miller.

Almost from the commencement of his career O'Neill has been recognized as an outstanding playwright; by 1930 it was apparent that he was the leading American dramatist and entitled to a place with the first dramatists of the new theater throughout the Western world. O'Neill has a unique combination of skill and vision: born and raised in the theater he is well-learned in the secrets of stage effect; years of travel and experience have given him a consciousness of the mystery of life which prevents him from using his skill merely for surface effect.

His earliest vignettes of the sailor's life suggest how his skill is to be made to serve the purposes of his vision. His father, James O'Neill, who destroyed his artistic career by yielding to the audience's thirst for sensation, would have been baffled by such a play as *Bound East for Cardiff,* although the violent action of its companion-piece, *Ile,* would have comforted him. *Bound East for Cardiff,* however, is a more direct statement of O'Neill's fundamental pessimism; the sailor dying against a background of his quarreling, disinterested mates is an image of the loneliness and frustration of man. The purpose of several of the one-act plays, like *Where the Cross Is Made* and *The Moon of the Carribees,* is the creation of atmosphere and mood, the action itself being incidental. And though the spectator is at once impressed by the life-likeness of the scene presented before him, he cannot long remain unconscious of revelations in depth to which the realistic drama was not always given.

O'Neill seems to visualize the process of living as a stream of consciousness in which the lifeline is always becoming fouled. He writes generally of normal life perverted, twisted, and rotted by some excess, mania, whim, or crank. As early as *Diff'rent* (1920), a major character announces that "Folks be all crazy and rotten to the core, and I'm done with the whole kit and caboodle of them." The playwright was not discouraged by his vision; rather he has continued to probe, to attempt to discover the motives of human conduct. His frequent choice of the sea or the farm as his background may be due to their symbolic value; life on shipboard as the world in miniature, the farm juxtaposing the order of nature and the disorder of man.

But in his mystical as well as in his realistic plays, O'Neill demonstrates the acute sense of form which was to make him an early leader of American expressionism. The structure of the play, the pattern of the action, even the shaping of the dialogue always follows a strict design, usually one devised for that particular play. The alternating settings of *Beyond the Horizon,* shifting from the open road to the interior of the farmhouse, parallel the choices which confront the two brothers in the action. The subtle changes in the realistic details of the setting, for the purposes of atmosphere and character interpretation, have already been commented on (p. 42). The reverse of this device is to be found in *All God's Chillun Got Wings,* where the fixed nature of the setting creates a dramatic symbol of the forces opposed to the self-realization of the hero and heroine. The basic setting here, in fact, is very close to pure expressionism:

A corner in lower New York, at the edge of a colored district. Three narrow streets converge. A triangular building in the rear, red brick, four-storied, its ground floor a grocery. Four-story tenements stretch away down the skyline of the two streets. The fire escapes are crowded with people. In the street leading left, the faces are all white; in the street leading right, all black. . . . One hears only their laughter. It expresses the difference in race. . . . From the side of the whites a high-pitched nasal tenor sings the chorus of "Only a Bird in a Gilded Cage." On the street of the blacks, a Negro strikes up the chorus of "I Guess I'll Have to Telegraph My Baby." As this singing ends, there is laughter, distinctive in quality, from both streets. Then silence.

All God's Chillun is not an expressionistic play. The characters and the action are realistically presented. It is an instance of O'Neill's willingness to extract symbolic values from his stage devices without regard for the possible destructive effect on the play's unity. In such a play as his masterpiece, *Mourning Becomes Electra,* the completely realistic setting is also completely symbolic. A part of the action takes place before the front of a carefully reproduced New England mansion of the "Greek revival" period. Since the plot revives a Greek myth, and since Greek tragedies were generally performed in the open area before a pillared temple-like structure, this setting aids in developing more than the literal meaning of the action.

In characterization, too, O'Neill prefers to follow a pattern. His characters are not necessarily stereotypes, but he is at some pains from early in his career to make sure that the relation of each character to his central theme or action shall be apparent. Later he was openly to employ real masks. In his early works he is willing to suggest the "humour" or manner of any one character by using the mask less literally. In *Beyond the Horizon,* for example,

Mrs. Mayo's face has lost all character, disintegrated, become a weak mask wearing a helpless, doleful expression of being constantly on the verge of comfortless tears.

In *The Great God Brown,* six years later, each character is equipped with a mask which he dons or doffs to indicate his inner nature, his attitude and his emotion. This is, perhaps, the logical outcome of a system of type characterization, but it wastes one of the theater's most valuable properties, the humanity of the actor. The general shuffling and exchanging, too, calls attention to the masks, away from the actors and the action, thus defeating the artist's intention of creating an organic whole. In *Mourning Becomes Electra*, where the Greek myth suggested the employment of actual masks, the realism of the New England setting forced O'Neill to compromise. The Mannons, in repose, all have masklike faces, resembling the masklike portraits on the walls of their library. But since the Mannons are rarely in repose, the effect is more potential than actual.

This use of the matériel of the theater, settings and make-up and action, on several levels achieves an effect similar to the effect of poetic language, and accounts for the impact of much of O'Neill's work in spite of the lack of poetic language in his dialogue.

Desire Under the Elms (1924) is a singularly effective example of the use of "theater poetry." The play tells a simple and terrible story. Ephraim Cabot, a tyrannical, hard-bitten, fundamentalist farmer has three sons: by his first wife, Simeon and Peter who dream of leaving the farm and joining the gold rush to California, and by his second wife, Eben who believes that Ephraim has worked his mother to death and resolves to avenge her. Eben steals money from Ephraim and gives it to his older brothers to get them on their way to the West, but as they leave Ephraim returns from a long absence with a third wife, the young and lusty Abbie. Abbie has married for security and she takes greedy possession of the farm. Eben resents this, since he feels the farm is by rights his, but he is as strongly attracted to Abbie as she to him. In the passionate conflict which follows, Abbie bears a son by Eben and then murders the child to prove to Eben that her love is real. It is not a pretty play, but it is almost overpowering on the stage as basic human emotions of passion and possession come into dramatic conflict.

The theme of the play is variations on the word *desire*. Abbie desires a home, security, Simeon and Peter desire freedom from the hard labor of a rock-bound New England farm, Eben desires to possess what was his mother's (with the obvious Freudian implication), and Old Ephraim desires to escape from his sense of aloneness by possessing the farm he has made out of impossible land, since human love fails him in each of his wives and in each of his sons.

Life on the farm has been a theatrical cliché for a hundred years, exploited by playwrights for sentimentality, low humor, and melodrama. What O'Neill has done is to examine the motive behind the affection for the Old Homestead: the desire to possess; he relates this desire to the animal desire to possess other things. The romance is gone when the motive is laid bare. But O'Neill goes farther. He demonstrates that the desire to possess grows out of a feeling of instability, of insecurity. Thus his picture of life is of a life without foundation, without creeds or beliefs, struggling for a symbol of security, a few rocky acres of a New England farmstead.

The abstract idea of desire is of course made concrete by the action, but the poetical use of the elements of the theater intensifies the concept. Over the farmhouse stand two elms bending heavily upon the roof. "They are like exhausted women resting their sagging breasts and hands and hair on its roof, and when it rains their tears trickle down monotonously and rot on the shingles." In the opening scene of Act II, the manner of the characters as they move heavily through the oppressive heat, their actions carefully guided by the author, even their voices, give the thematic word an almost physical presence. The disappearing wall of the farmhouse, permitting all rooms to be exposed at once, enables O'Neill to establish relationships and ironies visually, in terms of the theater. The play thus achieves an intensity and concentrated force common enough in the poetic drama but rare in the modern prose theater. Only because of its wider range does *Mourning Becomes Electra* surpass *Desire Under the Elms* in tragic vision. The two plays together represent the highest moments of the American drama.

The serious plays of Philip Barry, particularly *Hotel Universe* and *Here Come the Clowns,* identify him as O'Neill *in petto.* His great technical skill is evident in his social comedies, *Holiday, The Animal Kingdom, Paris Bound.* But in *Hotel Universe* (1930) he demonstrated that he was willing to use his skill to get beyond the gossip and scandal of the cocktail party and the problems of fashionable divorce.

The people involved are the typical social insects of the F. Scott Fitzgerald school, here set down in a typical playground of the bored rich, a Mediterranean villa. There is a suggestion of secondary meaning in the description of the setting: a terrace, almost triangular, against a backdrop of sea and sky, "like a wedge into space." Across this terrace, after dark, sweeps the beam of a near-by lighthouse, as old Stephen Field says, "like the Finger of God." But such comments and suggestions are only hints; the play begins in regulation high-comedy fashion, with conventional after-dinner coffee and equally conventional sarcasm. "All we've done for three mortal days," says one of the ladies, "has been to sit around and make bitter cracks about anything we could put our tongue to." The assembled characters are all nervous for they have witnessed a suicide which reminds four out of the six of their own contemplated self-destruction. Typically, some of the guests are drawn into a kind of parlor game in which they burlesque the supposed pompousness and business acumen of one of their number. At the end of the "act," one of the wives remarks, "I'm always afraid they'll slip over the line and turn into the people they're pretending to be." And so they do. In a moment the men are "acting" again, pretending to be children, and one by one the others come into it, involuntarily, until the scene ends in a fist fight in earnest.

Through the play wanders Stephen Field, mysterious father of the owner of the villa. He is the spokesman for Barry's philosophy:

I have found out a simple thing: that in existence there are three estates. There is the life of chairs and tables, of getting up and sitting down. There is the life one lives in one's imagining, in which one wishes, dreams, remembers. There is the life past death, which in itself contains the others. The three estates are one. We dwell now in this one, now in that—but in whichever we may be breezes from the others still blow upon us.

Stephen in that speech is also explaining the structure of the play, for Barry is presenting a dramatization of a series of states of mind, of conscious and subconscious life.

On the almost unlocalized platform, suspended in time and space, under the hypnotic effect of the rhythmic flashing of the lighthouse beam, or relaxed by sleeping powders, or elated by nervous tensions, the characters individually cross and recross the boundaries of the "three estates," or at least recognize the breezes that blow in upon them. As a result of the action, the disillusioned, the bitter, and the self-deluded are restored to sanity, to love of life and faith in man. "Am I right," asks Norman Rose at the end of the play, "in believing that some pretty funny business went on here tonight?" To which the heroine replies, "Well, I don't know if you'd call it funny—but suddenly everything seems possible.—It's like beginning all over again." Recalling the year of production, 1930, both the statement and the action were in themselves demonstrations of courage and faith. *Hotel Universe* is a fine and deeply moving play, although playing tricks with time and reality inevitably calls attention to ingenuity or trickery.

Eight years later Barry returned to serious drama with *Here Come the Clowns*. His characters now are the performers and hangers-on of a vaudeville house; in 1938 the rich had lost much of their conviction along with their wealth. But the story now is a kind of allegory of good and evil, and the characters are driven to reveal their innermost thoughts by an "illusionist," though under his spell their revelations are all of pain and frustration.

The allegory, not obvious enough to cause resistance, nor so obscure as to bewilder, is of man's search for God. Clancy, the "clown," is an ex-stagehand returned to the theater (the world) in search of James Concannon (God), the benevolent old manager who seems to be missing. If Concannon is not running the theater, who is? Perhaps it is Max Pabst (the devil), the illusionist, who can remark as he surveys the characters:

As fine a collection of wretched, unhappy human beings as ever it has been my privilege to behold. . . . The world in miniature—the variety-show *par excellence*—We cannot but regard it with pity. We must not be too amused.

Here Come the Clowns is in many ways Barry's most original play, a warm and pitying dramatization of the plight of the common man in a society without a moral rudder. Yet it never strays into sentimentality, it is never content with truth to the surface of life.

Both in *Hotel Universe* and *Here Come the Clowns* Barry is making effective use of the method of selective realism. Particularly in the latter play, where there is an obvious danger that the allegory might tyrannize over the playwright, the sense of actuality is never lost, yet the meaning of the action unfolds clearly as the action develops. The selective realist generally uses the theater more creatively than the simple realist, without going to the extremes of the expressionist. He does not design his action to interpret his symbols; rather, the symbols are intended to supplement the action. It is necessary to distinguish between such plays as *Desire Under the Elms* and *Here Come the Clowns* on the one hand and such as *The Great God Brown* and *The Adding Machine* (see pp. 96 ff.) on the other. The action of the first two plays is understandable to those who cannot or will not penetrate to the symbolic level; the action of the last two is incomprehensible until the meaning of the symbols has been established.

Perhaps the extreme limit of selective realism was reached in Arthur Miller's *Death of a Salesman* (1949). In *All My Sons,* Mr. Miller had buckled his play within the belt of rules, selecting and arranging his incidents in the manner of the well-made playwright and endowing certain of the properties used in the setting and action with symbolic value. *Death of a Salesman,* with its skeletal setting, non-realistic lighting, musical leitmotivs and free movement in time and space, suggests expressionism rather than realism; but these elements involve no distortion of reality. Miller is actually going a step beyond Ibsen in the use of delayed exposition (or retrospective action), but he does not go the whole distance to Strindberg or Kaiser.

In his great social dramas, Ibsen used delayed exposition to reveal gradually the events of the past as the present action developed, until at the climax of the play, the moment of greatest intensity in the action was also the moment of most complete revelation in the exposition. The effect was to show simultaneously the cause and the event, so that the theme became inescapable. Miller's innovation is in the direction of more complete visualization; what Ibsen was content to leave as narrative, information conveyed by the dialogue, Miller dramatizes.

His hero, Willy Loman, is an aging travelling salesman whose life has been founded on his beliefs that an attractive personality is the key to success in business and that one of his sons, who seems to possess such a personality, is destined to great achievement. Bewildered by both his own and his older son's failure to conquer the world, his mind begins to crack. Unbidden memories come back to him, and are acted out for the audience, memories of his brother Ben who made a fortune by the ruthless exploitation of "the jungle"; of his happy young manhood when his house was surrounded by trees instead of confined by apartment buildings, when he found satisfaction in making improvements in his property; of his father who went West selling flutes of his own manufacture; of his garden where he grew things before the encroaching city cut off the sunlight; of his son's youthful devotion; of the affair with the woman in Boston which turned his son against him.

Some of these recollections, of course, have symbolic value, are as much related to the theme of the play as to its action. But Willy never understands them, he only remembers. Thus, Ben appears in his habit as he lived, and the early years of Willy's marriage are presented as objectively as if they were the opening act of a chronologically arranged history. The comment must be made and the conclusions drawn by the audience on the basis of the juxtaposition of past and present. It is the audience that understands the connection between the scene in the Boston hotel and the desertion by the sons in the New York restaurant. To Willy it means nothing; for him the only connection is coincidence.

The symbolism of *Death of a Salesman* supplements the action, according to the normal procedure in selective realism. The meaning of the story, the reasons for the failure of Willy's life, is completely apparent in the action itself; the audience is not required to interpret a set of special symbols to arrive at comprehension. By refusing to sacrifice the sense of conviction that accompanies realism, Miller retains the immediacy of a social document. This undoubtedly explains in part the stunning effect of the play upon its audiences. A portion of commonplace experience moves before their eyes, and is given significance by the creative use of the devices of the theater.

Immediacy is *a* virtue, but it is not necessarily *all* the virtues, of drama. For Americans, and for societies similarly organized, *Death of a Salesman* is tragedy. For other societies it is a lesser thing, a case history, perhaps. It is questionable whether even the ablest of the selective realists has achieved universality in reflecting a world so full of chaos and contradiction. Yet universality does not cease to be a desideratum, at least for the critics, and it has led many a playwright on an exhausting and generally fruitless quest. The more successful of these playwrights have taken one of two roads: they have gone back to the beginnings to folk material, where manners were simpler and there was less differentiation between peoples; or they have sought the way of expressionism, creating a special, unique world for their action where everyday distinctions in manners and belief need not be appealed to. Both ways, of course, are eventually the way of poetry, of the completely creative use of the material available to the playwright.

4

FOLK DRAMA

THE return to folk materials in quest of universality is a characteristic of the international theater of the twentieth century. When W. B. Yeats and Lady Gregory were planning to establish a national tradition of theater in Dublin, they turned to folk, or as Yeats called it, "heroic" materials. A play, said Yeats, "should tell the people of their own life, or *the life of poetry* where every man can see his own image. To ennoble the man of the roads, write of the roads, or of people of romance, or the great historical people." Following his own precept, Yeats wrote principally of Cuchulain and Deirdre and similar figures out of, or related to, Irish legend. Other proponents of the folk movement, like Synge or the Spaniard García Lorca, have chosen to deal directly with the folk and the

unsophisticated motivations of inherited convention or natural belief. Still others, like the German Hauptmann, have
treated folk materials in terms of the naturalistic creed and
have demonstrated the principles of determinism in the
humblest situations.

Two problems confronted the would-be folk dramatist in
America. One obviously was to discover the "folk"; there
are so many and so dissimilar cultural patterns that it was
nearly impossible for any one to contain the desired universal elements. The second problem was one which had
confronted the Irish also: the folk characters who had
appeared in earlier drama had been treated as clowns, and
their entrance and their dialogue was a signal that the low
comedy portion of the evening had begun. As will be apparent in the discussion of American comedy (see p. 115), native
types quickly became established as comic figures, the
Yankee, the Negro, and so on.

A curious early example of the handling of folk materials in the popular theater is Frank Murdoch's thriller,
Davy Crockett, or *Make Sure You're Right Then Go Ahead*
(1872). Crockett, of course, was a historical figure, woodsman, fighter, and politician, and not unwilling to encour-
age the attempts to make something of a legend of himself
during his own lifetime. In the unimaginative way of the
professional man of the theater, Murdoch rejects both the
historical Crockett and the Crockett of received legend, and
invents a conventional romantic hero of the same name.
There is little to be said for the play, except for one stun-
ningly melodramatic incident. The material was there, and
the audience interest, but theatrical tradition was too
strong.

The early years of the twentieth century saw the experiments, in many dramatic forms and with many materials,

of Percy MacKaye. His adventure into folk drama (see *The Scarecrow*, p. 36) is deliberately a fantasy, achieving its universality by poetic means and requiring from the audience a suspension of disbelief rather than an intensification of the sense of truth. At about the same time James Herne was demonstrating that such characters as farmers, hitherto played only for laughter, could be treated seriously; there were also attempts to handle negroes, immigrants, and other stereotypes as something more than buffoons.

It was, however, many years before the professional theater attempted a story of "local color" told in dialect not intended for comic effect, with folk characters and customs respectfully drawn and regarded as an organic part of the whole play. One of the earliest was based on a theme echoing two of the recurrent convictions of the twenties, the evils of war and the hypocrisy of Christians. Hatcher Hughes set the scene of *Hell Bent fer Heaven* (1924) in the Carolina mountains, benefiting from a folk background that had become unusually familiar to Americans in general. The conflict is based on the most familiar aspect of that milieu, a feud, and the hero is derived (very much as in the case of *Davy Crockett*) from the current hero, Sergeant York, a mountaineer who fought in World War I and returned to find himself an American legend. Few dramatic actions are more ancient or recur more frequently than that involving a blood feud and revenge. Hughes doubles the conflict by making the real interest in his play the attempt of a woman to prevent a dead feud from being awakened by the machinations of the villain.

The villain, Rufe Pryor, is a real monster, a cowardly hypocrite who ruthlessly plays on the credulousness of the women folk with almost fatal results. He does not lack the co-operation of nature in his dastardly work, as a thunder-

storm, a bursting dam, and a flood all contribute to his
plot. There is, indeed, so much violence in the action, and
violence of a particularly familiar theatrical sort, that the
folk material seems to be little more than flavoring to make
the melodrama less stale.

There is a similar flaw in Lula Vollmer's famous *Sun-Up*
(1923). This too takes place in the Carolina mountains
and is concerned with the effect of the World War on the
mountaineers. The play begins as a picture of life, a record-
ing of customs and manners and attitudes. The older folk
are unable to understand the news of the war; they know
what it means to fight Yankees, or the government men—
but Huns? However, the Widow Cagle's son has some feeling of responsibility to his nation and enlists. He is killed
overseas. His death means nothing to his mother except
that "the Law" killed him, just as it had killed his father
during a raid on his illegal still.

The Widow finally sees the light when she gives shelter
to a young deserter, whom she protects because the Law is
against him. By a twist of the wrist of the long arm of
coincidence, it is revealed to her that the deserter's father
was the government man who killed her own husband. She
is about to shoot the young man when she hears the voice
of her dead son speaking to her of love and forgiveness; she
recalls that the deserter had a mammy too; and the rising
sun dispels the mists of ignorance and provinciality at the
moment of the falling curtain.

Both plays make use of folk material, but timidly, as if
they did not trust it. The reaction of the old hunter in
Hell Bent fer Heaven, as the returning soldier shows him
a German automatic pistol, suggests one of the possibilities
of folk drama. The old man pushes it aside, saying, "I
wouldn't be ketched dead in the woods with it." They ask

him to explain. "Because it's a insult to shootin'-men, that's why! It's built on the notion that you're a-goin' to miss all your fust shots!" However, the purpose of the scene is not local color or characterization but simply to plant the idea of the gun for use later in the action, in the manner of the well-made play.

Genuine folk drama has to be written from the inside out, as it were, from an interest in folk first and in theater second. This does not mean that the plays may not be theatrically effective; it does mean that theatrical effect will grow out of the material employed. The situation is similar to the re-creation of poetic drama in the modern theater; far too many playwrights have believed that the secret was to translate a conventional play into verse dialogue. But poetry is the spirit which must inform the whole; and so with the folk spirit, if the result is to be anything more than a conventional play or melodrama in an attractive or novel setting.

For that reason, since the commercial theater is not comfortable in fields of alien corn, folk drama was largely the creation of college and "little theaters" throughout the land, and they have remained its chief supporters. Perhaps this is as it should be, if the purpose of folk drama is to *tell the people of their own life* and thus make the theater once more a personal ritual experience instead of a time-passer merely. Since the Irish are a homogeneous nation, the plays of Synge could be produced in Dublin and be assured of an understanding audience. It hardly needs reiteration that America is far from homogeneous, and that her chief theatrical center, New York, mirrors her infinite variety. Many of the true folk plays have been produced in New York, but for short runs and to more or less special audiences. Only when one was decked out with the familiar enchantments of musical comedy, with songs and dances and vulgar jokes, as *Oklahoma!*, could it find a place in the commercial theater. And *Oklahoma!* was, as a critic noted, not folk but folksy. More original than the average musical, it was still phony; it was cute, like department store reproductions of Pennsylvania Dutchery.

One of the earliest impulses for the creation of true folk drama came from the enthusiasm of Frederick H. Koch, first at the University of North Dakota, later at the University of North Carolina. Under his guidance, his playwriting students explored the possibilities of the fresh story material to be found in their native regions. Although they were not concerned with the standards of the professional theater, many of their plays have proved remarkably durable upon the stage by freshness of setting, honesty of character, and strength of conflict. The most notable of these playwrights and the most original is the philosopher-poet, Paul Green, who made his first appearance with *The Last of the Lowries* (1920), a one-act melodrama about a gang of mountain outlaws.

Green shortly discovered his true métier in the treatment of the negro, whose mysticism and mixed comic and tragic sense of life was ideal subject matter for a poet. A series of one-act plays of negro life culminated in the writing of *In Abraham's Bosom,* a full-length tragedy which won the Pulitzer Prize for 1926. Undoubtedly much of the play's success with the general audience was due to its apparent preoccupation with a problem, for by 1926 the realistic drama had trained audiences to take problems in their stride. But Mr. Green's actual achievement is more original. *In Abraham's Bosom* is the first full-length play to capture the inner spirit of the negro. O'Neill's *Emperor Jones,* produced earlier, is actually concerned with man in general rather than the negro in particular.

Mr. Green tells of a mulatto, Abraham McCranie, who dreams of getting an education and escaping from the ignorance which holds his people in economic bondage. At every turn he is thwarted; not only are the whites against him, but his own race, governed by fear, refuses to help. In moments of tension, the passion and superstition which he endeavors to control overcome him. He cannot keep up his farm, he cannot hold a job in the city. In a final burst of anger he kills his half-brother, a white man, and is lynched. The action of the play is in fact nothing that Edward Sheldon might not have conceived as *The Nigger* twenty years before.

The manner, however, is nothing like Sheldon, or like the realistic or problem play. For the problem with which Green is concerned is not the conflict of white and black, but the problem of the negro himself, the conflict within. Abe's father was a white man and the white blood within him is at war with the black. If he comes to a tragic end, it is in a sense his own doing, not that of external forces opposed to him. The technique of the playwright establishes the point of attack in the opening scene.

The action of the scene takes place in a turpentine clearing in the Carolina woods during the noon rest hour. Three typical negroes are introduced, first with their work song, then laughing, singing, quarreling as they eat their lunch and dry the sweat from their bodies. Their concerns emerge in their speech: keeping in good with the white folks, eating well, bragging of the strength of their bodies. And always there are interspersed scraps of songs, hymns, spirituals, aimlessly, without cue or connection with the con-

versation. As they curl up to sleep off their meal, Abe enters
with an arithmetic book. Instead of eating his lunch he
figures away on a problem, and finally solves it with shouts
of triumph. His aim, he points out, is to open a school for
negro children, and every problem solved brings the school
nearer.

His father, the owner of the woods, enters with his white
son, Abe's half-brother. After a moment, Abe asks about
the prospects for the school. His question is turned aside,
but he persists. His half-brother threatens him, strikes him,
and Abe flies into a rage. In blind passion he knocks the
white youth down, for which his father punishes him with
a horsewhipping. As the white men leave, Abe's sweetheart
rushes in and, holding him in her arms, promises to take
him away into the woods to a cool place where she will make
love to him and make him forget his beating. In a kind of
trance he goes with her while the other workers clump about
the stage in a goatish revel.

A similar, and similarly effective, device for projecting
the two sides of Abe's nature is employed in Scene 2. He
has married and his wife has just borne the first of their
babies to live more than a day or two. Abe's whole devotion, however, is not to her, or to the child, or to his farm
work, but to his books which seem to him his sole hope
for salvation on earth. His wife and aunt speak of seeking
salvation in Jesus, but he brushes that aside as superstition;
this child too he is certain will die, for the Lord has no
concern with him. In the midst of his attempts to be ra-
tional, his white father enters to tell him that he has arranged for a negro grammar school to be established with
Abe as teacher, and has deeded to Abe the house in which
he lives and twenty-five acres of land. The effect of this
news is to liberate the emotional, passionate side of the

hero's nature. He abases himself before his wife and child, begs their forgiveness for his doubt, accuses himself of blasphemy. In a long rhythmical speech, punctuated by cries of "Yes, Lawd!" and "Jesus, Jesus," he throws himself on the mercy of Christ and concludes with the conviction that he has been saved. In a final ritual gesture, he baptizes his young son, "as if making an offering to some god."

One other scene in this remarkable tragedy may be singled out. At the end of his life, with success finally in his reach, Abe is betrayed by the duplicity of his worthless son. Frustration, as always, causes him to lose control of himself and he fights with some white men who are opposing him. As a result he is forced to flee from town, and while he is hiding in the fields he once more is confronted by his half-brother. He begs for help and is refused. In the struggle which follows, Abe kills the white man, and his emotions take complete control of him. The world reels about him, and the very trees seem to take on the forms of men. Stupefied, he watches a group of men walk by silently, in silhouette, dragging a negro with a rope about his neck; a lynching party remembered from his youth. A young negress and a young white dandy steal off amorously into the bushes; his mother and father. With a horrible cry of recognition he screams the same words that his fellow workers had called after him in the opening scene as he left with his sweetheart.

The success of *In Abraham's Bosom* as folk drama is thus based on quite different elements from its success as a realistic problem play. Mr. Green makes liberal use of rhythms, both in speech and action, which are peculiar to his material. The work song, the sexual dance, the religious chant: these convey not so much the *fact* of negro life as its *essence*. And these are in turn strengthened or set off by the cross rhythms of the white man and Abe's attempts to adopt another manner of living. In his later plays, Mr. Green has developed the use of rhythms and music into a form which he calls "Symphonic Drama." Of these, *Roll Sweet Chariot* (1934)[1] and *Tread the Green Grass* (1931) are original and effective, though perhaps more lyric than dramatic in their methods and aims. *The Field God* (1927) is a realistic drama of poor-white farmers, *The House of Connelly* (1931) combines the realistic treatment of a family of decaying Southern aristocrats with rhythmical interludes of negro life. The last play demonstrates, perhaps, how Mr. Green's handling of folk materials might find a place in the conventional theater. Big Sis and Little Sis, the two field women who form a chorus for his action, are at once images of the doom that hangs over the house, and symbols of the eternal rhythm of life which the Connellys have denied.

The most popular treatment of negro life on the American stage was of course the famous melodrama, *Uncle Tom's Cabin,* constantly played in various guises for nearly a century. Although intended as a serious treatment of the problem of slavery, it soon degenerated into a kind of variety entertainment on which any theatrical fad of the moment could be hung. *Tom's* only rival for popularity was a phenomenon of the nineteen-thirties, *The Green Pastures*. Dramatized by Marc Connelly from a series of stories by Roark Bradford, the play had enormous success both in New York and throughout the world.

The intention of the playwright was to present the spirit of the negro by analyzing one of his dominant traits, his intensely personal religious experience. We are introduced

1 Published in 1931 under the title, *Potter's Field.*

first to Mr. Deshee, a preacher, and his Sunday School class. The children pester him with questions about the world and God to which the Bible gives no specific answers. "De Book," he explains, "ain't got time to go into all de details." So Mr. Deshee undertakes to answer their questions in terms of his own experience and understanding. The play is a dramatization of his interpretation of the first books of the Bible.

The angels attend a fish fry in heaven and smoke ten-cent cigars. "Gangway for de Lawd God Jehovah!" cries Gabriel, as God enters dressed as a fine old negro minister to pass a miracle and create, incidentally, man. De Lawd goes for a long walk on His new earth, discusses life with Adam, watches the misbehavior of Cain with some misgiving, is relieved at the goodness of Noah, and constantly keeps Gabriel from blowing his horn. We watch Noah arguing the virtues of two kegs of liquor as ballast for the ark, and Moses doing magic tricks for old King Pharaoh in the lodge rooms of the Mystic Brothers of the Egyptian Home Guard, and the King of Babylon passing out pecks of rubies to his dancing girls.

The student of the drama is instantly reminded of the old English craft cycles, the long plays in many parts dramatizing scenes from biblical history in terms comprehensible to their uneducated spectators: Herod surrounded by his "knights," the shepherds who visit the Christ Child bringing him gifts appropriate to a new-born English baby. But there is an important difference in intention if not in method between the craft cycle and *The Green Pastures*. The anachronisms in the medieval plays were for the purpose of communication, to make plain the meaning of the stories. *The Green Pastures* is not concerned with the meaning of the stories it retells so much as with the manner of their retelling.

Connelly's work may best be compared with the elaborate arrangements of negro spirituals so common in musical performances. Whatever significance the original may have had for its inventor or its singers is lost in the mechanics of harmonics and setting. True, the sincerity of the actors and the nature of the subject tended to impose a certain soberness on the audience, but the total effect was tinged with the sense of the quaint. That is to say, once again, that the folk elements are more decorative than functional.

But the negro is not the only source of folk materials for the American drama. Alexander Drummond, at Cornell University, has developed with his students a repertory of plays based on the lore and legend of New York State; at the University of Iowa, at Wisconsin, and in various communities of the West and Southwest a vigorous tradition of local color theater has been established. These plays cannot confine themselves to racial groups as in Carolina, for often no such groups of any significant size are available; they cannot confine themselves to legendary heroes, for the supply of John Henrys and Paul Bunyans is limited. They have therefore turned away from the matter of Yeats and Synge, the unsophisticated "folk," to the typical citizens of their areas, the farmers or workers or criminals. The result has been an increase in the production of realistic drama, although, since it is always in terms of the special reality of its audience, it retains much of the immediacy of the pure folk drama.

One subject and one hero, however, is almost inevitable in any of these local theaters. Sooner or later their playwrights get around to Abraham Lincoln whose legendary history is as valid for most Americans as his actual biography. He has, of course, been the subject of, or an actor in, a great many of the successful plays of the commercial theater, most notably Robert E. Sherwood's *Abe Lincoln in Illinois* (1938). The best of the more imaginative treatments is E. P. Conkle's *Prologue to Glory,* produced first in Iowa, then by the Federal Theatre in New York in 1938.

Mr. Sherwood follows the way of history, deriving much of his dialogue from the actual words of the persons as recorded in the diaries and papers of the time. Mr. Conkle on the other hand frankly admits that "This play makes no attempt to be true in all its historical details; it attempts rather to be true to the spirit of the times and the leading character." Both playwrights are concerned with the same theme: how a character like Lincoln's in his youth could be developed into that of the wise political and moral leader of a nation in crisis. Conkle confines himself to the New Salem years, Sherwood ends with Lincoln's departure for Washington.

Sherwood's play is obviously painted on a larger canvas. He portrays in some detail the many influences that were at work on his hero: his friends, his wife's ambition, his own vision of good. And since none of these is really sufficient to provide the peripeteia in Lincoln's life, he invents a touching scene on the prairie where his neighbor's faith in him restores his faith in himself. In the framework of the play, the invented scene is wholly convincing, but it is the creation of a literary biographer concerned with the complexities of his chosen hero.

Conkle's Lincoln is the Lincoln of legend and folklore. We see him at work, and avoiding work, and in love, and at play. He speaks, not the language of the Douglas debates or that in which his famous stories have been recorded, but the language of the Middle Border. He is the shrewd, lazy, lovable Abe that Americans like to consider a kind of national symbol. And it does not make him less appealing theatrically to demonstrate that at nearly every turn he was guided or impelled towards greatness by the women in his life. The play is true not merely to the spirit of its own times but of all times, as Americans are given to see the times. It is thus an illustration of Yeats' principle that the people might be enlightened by writing of "the great historical people," and in their own terms, rather than the terms of historians or serious biographers.

Such handling of folk material does not exploit the folk to its fullest extent, dramatically, since it is colored by other interests. For pure folk drama, without the suggestion of social problems or national propaganda, we may consider the work of Lynn Riggs in such plays as *Green Grow the Lilacs* (1931), the source of *Oklahoma!*, and *Roadside* (1930). The latter, which might be described as the great American comedy, fashions out of completely indigenous materials a statement of the concept of freedom which more than any other may be said to be held in common by all the otherwise differentiated races and classes and social groups that make up the country.

Roadside is a kind of tall story about Tall Stories, using the folk material of Southwestern America. Significantly, the action is dated 1905, but the matter goes back much farther; it is related to Davy Crockett, and Paul Bunyan, and Mike Fink, and the Jumping Frog of Calaveras County, and the story of the man who pulled a mountain lion inside out. It draws a picture of that vanished state of innocence when men lived close to nature and behaved with some of nature's prodigal exuberance. Hannie, the heroine, explains to her divorced husband how she came to marry him:

All I c'n recollect was once about two year ago· it was Spring, and Pap and me stopped by that little branch that run th'ough yore cow pasture. And you come down to set the dogs on us. When you seen me—you didn't. So I fell in a daze er sump'n— and when I come to, it seemed like I was kinda married to you—All on account of it bein' Spring, and you not settin' the dogs on us—and one other thing. I was all set to marry *someone* along about then—and I never thought to be picky and choosy.

Texas, the hero, is the very symbol of the untamed in his behavior and in his speech. His speech is as prolific as a rabbit, as irresponsible as a colt. He is the freedom-loving man, the child of nature, unhappy in civilization, happy along the "road," and the very manner of his speech, while characteristic of the ring-tail roarer of Western folk literature, is even more a verbalization of his natural instinct, free, irresponsible, violent, ecstatic. The story of his birth is a fantasia after the manner of Western guides, but it is more than a story to him; he believes it, almost.

What distinguishes this play from the usual melodrama about the West is obviously the freshness and poetry of the speech, and the warm humanity of the characters. But a more important distinction is the idea, the theme, which is at its core. It is a very serious theme, however lightly it may be treated, and one of equal pertinence in Texas' world and ours. The date of the action is important. The year 1905 was not the year of Bunyan and Fink and Crockett. It was the year of the railroad and the farm. Civilization was settling down on nature. Buzzy, the farmer, is training and controlling the natural processes of the earth as the Marshal is training and controlling the natural instincts of men. Any of the real folk heroes would have challenged the Marshal to shoot him, and caught the bullet in his teeth. But Texas has to submit before armed might.

Texas can only get the better of the Marshal when he is unarmed, when his back is turned, or when he can "talk him over" by appealing to the fundamental human instinct for freedom which is in him too, in spite of his badge, his profession, and his veneer of urbanization. When Texas drives off with Hannie in the final scene, crying, "Good-bye, you all, bet you wish you was us," the Marshal waves good-bye with his handkerchief, with an admiring grin. *—note*

Roadside is about liberty, the liberty of individuals, about human importance and dignity. This is a subject with which modern drama has often been preoccupied, but often in terms more didactic than dramatic. By turning to folk materials, which can be felt more than intellectually comprehended, Riggs appeals to the instinct dormant in most Americans to live close to nature. He thus states his theme by indirection, by character in action awakening the nostalgia of his audience. It is not only the Marshal who grins admiringly in reply to Texas' farewell, "Bet you wish you was us!"

5

BEYOND THE FOURTH WALL

FTER the American theater tardily recognized the spirit of realism which inspired the new drama of Europe, it matured and expanded rapidly. In the twenties it was regularly surpassing in quality and seriousness those theaters that had been its mentors. During the years from 1920 to 1950 there were few playwrights from abroad to contest the superiority of such Americans as O'Neill, Barry, Howard, and Sherwood in the drama of realism.

However, by 1910, realism was no longer the be-all of the modern continental theater. A new spirit was developing which threatened to replace it completely—expressionism. This is a term covering a variety of approaches and devices, but in general it may be described as the subjective rather than the objective presentation of dramatic narrative, resulting in a play in which the symbol tends to dominate the action. Beginning with the experiments of August Strindberg at the end of the nineteenth century, it was fostered by the symbolic technique of Maurice Maeterlinck. Its great impulse, however, came in Germany during and shortly after the first World War when playwrights discovered that the older realism and its concomitant well-made-play form was totally unsuited to a society in a state of collapse. Gradually these playwrights developed a form to which distortion was the key: grotesque exaggeration in setting, costume and make-up, each detail symbolically significant, and the whole mass signifying— nothing, if it was that kind of play; everything, if it was another type.

Expressionism was not so much a prescribed form or convention as a crystallization of the spirit of the age. Its earliest American manifestation, in the work of Eugene O'Neill, came without any prompting from the European pioneers. In his desire to escape from the "banality of surfaces," O'Neill wrote *The Emperor Jones* (1920) employing some of the devices of expressionism, "long before I had ever heard of expressionism."

The form of *The Emperor Jones* is organic to the matter and intention. They were conceived together, and the meaning of the play is as implicit in the structure as it is made explicit in the dialogue. *Jones* is, of course, not only one of the most famous of American plays, but it has had a longer stage life than most dramas deliberately written according to the formulas of expressionism. One reason for this is certainly that which has given even O'Neill's failures a certain validity: his instinctive, or perhaps inherited, knowledge of the theater and the devices available to the playwright. In *Jones,* for instance, he employs an elaborate scenic plan, demands a complex lighting system, and introduces spectacular costumes and masks. But these are not employed for their own beauty and effectiveness, to create a spectacle or decorate the performance; they are an integral part of the theme of the play; they are, in every instance, symbolic.

Brutus Jones is the self-appointed ruler of a small Caribbean state, where at the beginning of the play the natives are led by a witch doctor to rise against him. Superb in his uniform, confident of himself as a civilized man, he sets out to follow a carefully planned route through the jungle to safety, taking as a precaution a silver bullet with which to commit suicide if events should go against him. As scene succeeds scene, as he moves from one to another place in the jungle, he becomes more and more desperately lost, and in his increasing terror, he begins to see visions of his past and of the past of his race—as pullman porter, slave, superstitious aborigine. Each element of the past asserts its hold upon him more firmly, until in the final scene he is writhing in insane terror before a primitive god, naked, hardly able to speak or reason. He fires his pistol for the last time, and his dead body is found by the insurgent natives only a few miles from his starting point.

The whole action is an allegory of man's inability to escape from his past—not just his immediate past, his own experience, but from the heritage of all men, the "little nameless fears," the primitive urges that overpower reason, civilization, sophistication, in moments of crisis. Any single dramatic device that O'Neill uses to present this allegory may be tracked to its place among the conventions of the older theater; the novelty lies in its integration with the play's theme, and its demonstrated ability to draw the audience into the experience. Even the incessant, increasingly rapid beat of the tom-toms which runs through the play and is one of its most famous features is in essence the "hurry music" and other leitmotivs so characteristic of melodrama. But again, as in the case of the other theatrical devices, it is not simply an added ornament to the production but bound up in the statement of its theme.

The writing of *The Emperor Jones* demonstrated to O'Neill that escape from fourth-wall realism was possible. In *The Hairy Ape* (1922) he continued to experiment with the possibilities of symbolic techniques. The most notably expressionistic devices here are to be found in the settings which, to be sure, suggest actual locales, but the suggestion is so distorted that the effect is an interpretation rather than a presentation. Some hint of this use of scenery is in the stage directions quoted from *Beyond the Horizon* (see p. 42), where rooms are furnished to hint at the character of the occupants. The symbolism, however, if present, is subordinated.

In *The Hairy Ape,* the symbolism of the setting becomes inescapable. The stokehold is obviously a stokehold, but it also suggests a prison or a cave; the deck of the ship suggests, in addition, sterility; the New York street suggests a way of life whose values are purely material. Each of these symbols contains some part of the meaning of its scene, and the sum of them is on one level the theme of the total play.

The hero, Yank, has been thoughtlessly contented with his lot in life. At the beginning of the play, an intruder from the outer world encourages the faint glimmer of doubt that his may not be the best of all possible worlds, arouses in him discontent and a sense of homelessness. He sets out in quest of his home, of the place where he "belongs." This quest involves him, and O'Neill, for the first time with masked characters. The wealthy churchgoers are a choral caricature of the social-materialistic successful men and women: their mask-like faces, puppet-like gestures, and unison movements express their natures without words or commentary and in terms consonant with the total concept of the play.

In *The Great God Brown* (1926) O'Neill continued the use of a symbolic setting and further exploited the possibilities of masked actors. There are few more difficult or obscure plays in the repertory of American drama; but the obscurity is inherent in the matter, not the method. O'Neill is trying to invoke the mystery of the whole of existence, spiritual and material, to present not a key to the mystery but the mystery itself. The many scenes of the play, for instance, are given a unity by the arrangement of furniture or properties within them. In all except the double scenes, the furniture is placed in a square ⌐⌐ with the open end facing the audience. The purpose of this arrangement is indicated by a stage direction in the Prologue: *Billy stands at the left corner, forward, his hand on the rail, like a prisoner at the bar, facing the judge.* The repetition of this symbolic setting and the relationship of the characters within it—Brown facing his father on the level of material success, Dion facing God on the level of the spiritual quest, Margaret facing the Moon on the level of the life force— composes a picture of Man on trial before a judge he can neither see nor imagine.

The masks are a perhaps overly-explicit device for conveying the notion of the secret self, that there is one face for the public and another for ourselves. Dion's mask is a "fixed forcing of his own face—dark, spiritual, poetic . . . into the expression of a mocking, reckless, defiant, gaily scoffing, and sensual young Pan"; his experiences in the play gradually change Pan into Mephistopheles. It is this mask-aspect that Margaret loves. She does not recognize, or love, the real man beneath, the Christian ascetic and poet, St. Antony. Nor is she completely happy in her love until the worldly successful William Brown acquires the mask of Dion (Dionysus) and becomes the perfect combination: materialistic, yet romantically attractive in the false sense of the old-fashioned actor (James O'Neill?) to whom the playwright directly refers during the rape of Margaret in the Prologue.

Modern man searches for love ("to belong" in Yank's terms), but the older, traditional sources of love are cut off: the family, the wife, God. Only Cybel can assert with authority, "Our Father who art." She tries to inspire Dion with her own certainty of the importance of living for the sake of life. As the symbol of the Earth Mother, she is doomed to segregation in a world of laws made by men seeking other goals; she does not struggle, she accepts. The others die in their desperate search for meaning: Cybel exists, as does Margaret, who acknowledges the same eternal power. *The Great God Brown* thus becomes a theatrical image of the frustration of modern man, using all the resources of the stage as well as of the playwright to convey its sense of mystery and affirmation:

Always spring comes again bearing life! Always again! Always, always forever again!—Spring again!—life again!—summer and fall and death and peace again! But always, always, love and conception and birth and pain again—spring bearing the intolerable chalice of life again!—bearing the glorious, blazing crown of life again!

Perhaps because of its rejection of the more conventional form of the well-made play, expressionism has been widely

employed by dramatists whose primary intention was a
criticism of the social order. In *The Adding Machine* (1923)
Elmer Rice drew one of the most penetrating and most
critical of the many portraits of the "little man" so popular
in the drama of the twenties. His central figure, Mr. Zero,
is presented without sentiment and, in a sense, without
mercy: a nameless, characterless, thoughtless victim of the
machine age, compounded of the "unnecessary letter," and
"an o without a figure." By distorting the objects of his
play, the settings, characters and properties, Rice contrives
a picture of the world as it appears to Mr. Zero, a book-
keeper. His parlor walls are papered with sheets of foolscap
bearing columns of figures, the doorbell clicks like an adding machine; his neighbors, "all shapes and sizes," are
dressed exactly alike, and all like Zero. Devices of the theater are used to project Zero's personal reactions, to make
concrete his emotional responses to situations. When his
nameless Boss announces with callous rhetoric that Zero
is fired, the sound of a mechanical band on a merry-go-
round is heard and the stage begins to revolve. The Boss, at
Zero's request, repeats his statement, then:

*His voice is drowned by the music. The platform is revolving
rapidly now. Zero and the Boss face each other. They are
entirely motionless save for the Boss's jaws, which open and
close incessantly. But the words are inaudible. The music swells
and swells. To it is added every off-stage effect of the theater:
the wind, the waves, the galloping horses, the locomotive whis-
tle, the sleighbells, the automobile siren, the glass crash, New
Year's Eve, Election Night, Armistice Day, and the Mardi Gras.
The noise is deafening, maddening, unendurable. Suddenly it
culminates in a terrific peal of thunder. For an instant there
is a flash of red and then everything is plunged into blackness.*

Zero has killed the Boss.

The Adding Machine is not so much an attack on the social or economic order as a satire on those who might be called the "victims" of the machine. After his execution, Zero discovers that his troubles have just begun. He meets another ghost who informs him that the torments of eternity await all murderers, but this appears to him to be old-fashioned fundamentalist nonsense. In the course of his visit to Heaven, however, he discovers that the machine age is completely equipped with a machine theology. He is trained to run the latest type of adding machine and sent back to earth to start all over again. There is, perhaps, nothing new in Rice's social criticism, but the devices of expressionism give a freshness to the ideas which makes them seem important to an audience inclined to ignore the truth in truisms.

Two plays from the twenties by John Howard Lawson show the playwright using expressionism increasingly to develop a less moderate criticism of society. In the first, *Roger Bloomer* (1923), Lawson dramatizes the adolescence of a young Midwesterner as he frees himself from the conventions of his childhood and faces the uncertainties and unanswerable questions of maturity. The play incorporates a dream sequence in the form of a symbolic ballet, and makes use of skeleton settings, "space staging," and special curtains to suggest the atmosphere of each of the major locales. The action flows back and forth across the stage like the intercut scenes of a movie, yielding the same impression of movement, of panorama, of the *whole* truth.

Processional, presented by the Theatre Guild in 1925, is described by Lawson as "a jazz symphony of American life." For his form he turned to vaudeville, a kind of theatrical entertainment which seemed, in 1925, to express the state of the nation in a native idiom. He wrote:

It is only in the fields of vaudeville and the revue that a native craftsmanship exists. . . . Here the national consciousness finds at least a partial reflection of itself in the mammy melody, the song and dance act and the curtain of real pearls. Here the concern is with a direct contact, an immediate emotional response across the footlights.

Following the conventions of vaudeville, the opening scene is a typical "street drop," with houses and advertisements painted in perspective. The characters are the recognizable stereotypes of the two-a-day. The heroine's father is Mr. Cohen, a deliberate caricature in speech, actions, and appearance. Hiram Phillpotts, the juvenile, is described as "young, amiable, brisk, neat made-to-order clothes, straw hat, nasal voice, folding kodak flung over shoulder, a very George M. Cohan sort of a newspaper man," and his entrance is accompanied by a nasal voice singing on a phonograph,

> There is no land as great as my land
> From California to Manhattan Island. . . .

The tone of the play ranges from burlesque to tragic. As the sheriff is reading the charges against Dynamite Jim, a collapsible chair breaks under him; a highly sentimental discussion of mother love takes place against a background of a prostitute singing in "The Temple of Labor"; a serious scene between Jim and his mother in their make-shift home is deliberately broken as Cohen and a newsboy "erupt" into it, the newsboy swallowing evidence in the tradition of melodrama, Sadie Cohen dancing with another character in the manner of a song-and-dance team. Capitalism, the Ku Klux Klan, the rights of Labor, the venality of the Law, all find a place in what appears to be the lavish hodgepodge of a variety show, but is actually a serious political document. Although the next decade was to give birth to a series of proletarian dramas—John Wexley's *They Shall Not Die,* Albert Maltz' *The Black Pit,* Clifford Odets' *Waiting for Lefty,* and others—and even to an organization, The Theatre Union, dedicated to their production, *Processional* alone, by reason of its skillful use of the theater retains some of the vitality of genuine art.

Later playwrights have made creative use of the devices of the theater not for propaganda but to achieve universality. After a series of experiments with the one-act play, Thornton Wilder wrote *Our Town* (1938), a touching picture of life in a New England community. By abandoning scenery, performing his simple story of birth and marriage and death against the bare walls of the stage, he was endeavoring to revive some of the ability of the Elizabethan theater to lend importance to the actor who, perhaps, had been rather dwarfed by the mechanical splendors with which the realistic stage had surrounded him. The production plan was well adjusted to the homeliness of the action and the characters; the play is totally void of sensationalism, yet it took its place at once in the standard repertory of the American theater, as a kind of celebration of the humble. Not wholly devoid of sentimentalism, it is rarely whimsical and never cute.

Wilder's second play, *The Merchant of Yonkers* (1938), was a further experiment in the uses of the theater. Here he frankly employs the plot and devices of a Middle-European farce of a type wholly forgotten by the twentieth century. His purpose seems to have been to see what could be made of the rejected convention of the soliloquy, which he revives not to reveal the inner thoughts of the characters (like O'Neill in *Strange Interlude),* but to introduce philosophical disquisitions growing out of the action and situations. The method is completely unrealistic, as one by one the major characters step to the footlights and speak the author's mind. The original presentation of *The Merchant* was a failure, largely because of a heavy-handed production; the device still awaits its justification.

The Skin of Our Teeth (1942) is in many ways Wilder's most creative use of the theater. His theme is the survival of the human race in the face of ignorance, catastrophe, and folly, and he moves backward and forward in time with disconcerting (some critics said Joycean) rapidity. The play opens in the typical fashion of Victorian farce with a soliloquy by a pert chambermaid, but before long the walls of the room are leaning at crazy angles, Homer and the Muses and a baby mammoth are seeking shelter from the approaching icecap, the audience is urged to contribute its chairs to a fire to save the race from refrigeration. The form of the play admits a convention of mammals at Atlantic City, the transformation of the chambermaid into Lilith and a camp follower, and a pageant of Great Philosophers. For sheer variety and mingling of emotions, it is to be compared only to *Processional,* but its theme is a celebration rather than a criticism of humanity. Like the symbolism of O'Neill in *Desire Under the Elms* this creative use of familiar material and conventions comes very close to creating a poetry of the theater.

Of the younger writers, none has been more dedicated to theatrical symbolism than Tennessee Williams. In three plays produced before 1950, *The Glass Menagerie* (1945), *A Streetcar Named Desire* (1947), *Summer and Smoke* (1948), he writes of the South of which he is a native. Invariably his central figure is a woman, and always as a standard for her conduct there is in her background the code of genteel behavior celebrated in ante-bellum romance. One by one these women, since their code has no relation to the world in which they have lost themselves, come to grief: a widowed mother, believing that woman's sole duty is to marry, drives her crippled daughter to a humiliating rebuff; upon an elder daughter, raised in the tradition of frailty and helplessness, devolves the crushing weight of a bankrupt plantation; a pallid notion of the life of culture and refinement cuts off a young girl from the normal happiness to which she is entitled. In each case, objectively considered, the lives of the heroines are failures, frustration leads to immorality, perversion, or insanity. Yet Williams sees them, in the end, through their own eyes, subjectively, as they find refuge in illusion, and comfort in their dreams and visions.

Thus, though his themes are in possibility tragic, his plays are in actuality pathetic. Each of his characters passionately resists the moment of illumination, rejects the self-knowledge which might give tragic dignity to her failure. However, true pathos, growing out of the author's sympathetic understanding rather than his sensibility, is almost as rare a quality in the drama as tragedy, and it may be that the substitution of psychiatry for morality as a basis for evaluation has effectively eliminated the possibilities for tragedy in the contemporary theater. Yet the constant elements in Mr. Williams' plots, the dead hand of tradition, illusion, collapse, could be united into a tragic theme of universal significance.

The playwright chooses to give importance to the particular, the unique, rather than to the universal. The story of Blanche DuBois in *A Streetcar:* her education to a tradition that was remote from the actual world and a mockery on the no-longer self-sufficient family plantation, her un-

fortunate marriage with the accompanying shock of perversion and suicide, her drifting into alcoholism and
nymphomania, and finally the confrontation with her
brother-in-law, ruthless, amoral, without illusions—all this
reads like a case history with no meaning beyond an analysis of one instance of human frailty. But the action of the
play is enveloped in symbolism: the walls of the room dis-
solve to reveal action on the street outside echoing or antici-
pating the action within, jazz music from a saloon piano
alternates with the remembered strains of a string ensemble
playing a ballroom dance. By such devices the situation is
enlarged, taken out of place and time, presented as a facet
of the mystery of humanity.

The smallest details of the action also bear their symbolic weight. Blanche covers the electric bulbs with colored
paper shades, just as she tells fantastic lies, not to shut off
the light, the truth, but to modify it until it can be tolerated. "I'll tell you what I want," she cries, "Magic! Yes, yes,
magic! I try to give that to people. I misrepresent things
to them. I don't tell truth, I tell what *ought* to be truth.
And if that is sinful, then let me be damned for it!" Even
the bathroom, which figures prominently in the action, has
its symbolic uses, as it reflects the vulgarity and earthiness
of the hero while serving Blanche as a place of retreat and
escape. These symbols have all been successfully absorbed
into the action; it is not necessary to be aware of their
meaning to experience the full impact of the play.

The danger of symbolism, as with other expressionistic
devices, is the risk of obviousness. The masks of *The Great
God Brown* force the audience to consciousness of the
mechanics of the play, where the merest suggestion of masks
in *Mourning Becomes Electra* emphasizes the idea of the
inherited evil without stepping over the confines of art into

didacticism. One of the causes for the failure of Mr. Williams' *Summer and Smoke* was surely his insistence upon the symbolism of his symbols. When the heroine, Alma, is forced to listen to a lecture on anatomy and is challenged to discover the location of the soul (it has been pointed out that "Alma" means "soul") on a chart of the human body, the spectator rustles uncomfortably and remembers his own efforts as poet laureate of the junior class at Central High School. Blanche's alcoholism is so commonplace a symbol of escape that it can be accepted without thought; Alma carries about with her a box of sleeping pills.

On the other hand, the successful use of symbolism, the free employment of the devices of the theater unrestricted by the attempted realism of the "fourth wall," has led to the creation of some of the most durable and vital plays of the modern repertory. Properly handled, organically related to the action and purpose of the whole work, the devices of expressionism have permitted playwrights to penetrate beneath the surface of their situations, to reveal truths which realism by its nature tends to disguise. This penetration, this revelation of inner truth, brings the contemporary drama once more into a close relationship with the great repertory of the poetic drama of the past. If such men as O'Neill and Tennessee Williams write dialogue in the prose convention, their use of the physical aspects of the theater—scenery, the actors' persons, properties—is creative and poetic.

The American theater is too much a creation of the twentieth century to have given much encouragement to the playwright who wishes to employ poetic dialogue. There have been attempts, doomed to fail on the stage, or at best to succeed as closet drama in the library. Only Maxwell Anderson, whose long career in the theater has embraced everything from *What Price Glory?* to musical comedy, has clung doggedly to his conviction that the drama of importance will be drama of poetic expression. Prose, he once announced, was a suitable language for information, but poetry was the language of emotion. The limitations of such a definition of poetry in the drama become apparent after an examination of Mr. Anderson's campaign to restore elevation of diction and high seriousness to the modern theater.

He began by modelling his work on that of the great Elizabethans, choosing characters and settings from remote history, retelling the stories of Queen Elizabeth, Mary Queen of Scots, and Crown Prince Rudolph. In *Elizabeth the Queen* (1930) and *Mary of Scotland* (1933) he achieved considerable success in giving stage life to historical portraits, humanizing the departed great by revealing that they too were unhappy in love. *The Masque of Kings* (1937), based on the Mayerling mystery, also treats of love in high places, but attempts to make some comments on kingship and democracy that will have significance for a contemporary American audience.

Mr. Anderson's notion of the nature and function of poetry in the drama is apparent in his first romantic plays. *Elizabeth the Queen* is shot through with Shakespeareanisms, not only in obvious references, like the Queen's greeting to Essex ("Ill-met by moonlight"), but in the employment of a Fool. But the Fool here is not functional as in *King Lear,* where he bears the burden of truth; Elizabeth's Fool reads like a Victorian critic's essay on the pathetic nature of the fool on the heath. For all the elegance of the language, too, the action is often theatrical cliché. In parting, Elizabeth gives Essex a ring, promising that if ever she is angry with him, the ring will restore him to favor; a method of plot development at least as old as Menander. Again, while Elizabeth is grieving over Essex's apparent desertion of her, the actors from the public theater play before her a scene from *Henry IV, Part I*. While this is highly effective theatrically, it should be noted that it is but an intellectualized treatment of the ancient motif of smiling-through-tears.

In the *Masque of Kings,* whose setting is the Middle Europe of a thousand romantic operettas, the tendency to Elizabethan diction and actual echoes of Shakespeare continues, with less fortunate results. It is possible, that is, for Queen Elizabeth to have been so struck by *A Midsummer Night's Dream* that a phrase or two might creep into her casual conversation. But it is startling to hear the Austrian Crown Prince protest, "What in God's name is Taafe to you that you should plead for him?" The dialogue of this play, the poetry, is about equally divided between facile cynicism and extended passages assembling a multitude of simple images. Of the functional image or the developed or repeated metaphor there is little use. Nor is there much attempt to distinguish among the characters by the manner of their poetry, their vocabulary. The spectator can sympathize with old Franz Josef when he says, after a series of lectures from his son, "And now indeed I understand you, though your flux of figures takes some unravelling."

Winterset (1935) is both an advance and a retreat. It was surely a worthy decision to get his characters out of costume, boldly to meet his audience in its own terms. The highly symbolic, but at the same time recognizably realistic setting, makes functional use of the theatrical tools at the playwright's disposal. The theme of the nature of justice and revenge is both immediate, growing out of a social problem, and eternal, of concern to all men and all times. Even the choice of the well-made play as a dramatic form is a courageous innovation, free as it is from the glaze of the antique, from the suggestion of being a part of a revival.

The recollections of Shakespeare, however, are inescapable. Seventeen-year-old Mio meets fifteen-year-old Miriamne at a dance and falls in love with her without knowing that there is a barrier between their families. The boy is seeking revenge for the death of his father whose voice still cries out from the quicklime in which he was buried. The old judge, who had condemned Mio's father, goes insane and sings dirty songs, and conducts a mad trial while a thunderstorm rages in the background. At the end of the play, the young lovers commit suicide in order to die together. These echoes of *Romeo* and *Hamlet* and *Lear* are not in themselves to be condemned. Originality in plotting is the least valuable of dramatic gifts; the use which the dramatist makes of his legitimate borrowings is the thing.

Mr. Anderson uses them for stage effect. The major theme on which he embarks is never developed by the action. Mio's quest for revenge for the injustice done his father is turned by his love for Miriamne into a desire to forgive. As a result of this change of heart, or growth of heart, he dies. Old Esdras, Miriamne's father and the chorus character of the play, is completely negative. "You're young enough to seek the truth," he points out, "and there is no truth." All the fury of the action, the passionate love, the walking corpse, the mad trial, ends in a burst of gunfire and silence. Old Esdras makes a rhetorical declaration over the bodies of his daughter and her beloved that it is the glory of man to struggle and never to yield. But as to the object of the struggle and the nature of the opponent he is rhetorically vague. The action, disassociated from the theme, becomes melodrama, to which the poetry of the dialogue is a coat of many colors and no pertinence.

Joan of Lorraine (1946) suggests that Mr. Anderson may have enlarged his definition of dramatic poetry to something more than the language of emotion. Here he is both telling a modern story and retelling an ancient one, drawing his theme from the parallels in his "double plot." From the life of Joan of Arc he selects a series of incidents illustrating the practicality of utilizing the forces of evil to achieve a good end. This is presented as a rehearsal of a historical play on a bare stage, with the actors only partly in costume, and with the action continually interrupted by the distractions that rehearsals are heir to. The leading lady objects vigorously to her role; she does not believe that Joan's career proves what the author means it to prove. The production is having money trouble; a principal backer is a criminal, the self-interest of union labor threatens catastrophe, even corruption in the box office becomes an issue. As the modern action develops it becomes apparent to the actress that these evil forces of crime, self-interest and immorality must be dealt with, must be used that the greater good, the creation of a work of art, may be served.

The play is thus a more successful attempt to restore poetic theater. It makes creative use of the resources of the stage, the mechanics of the stage house are adapted to the play, the play is not forced into a conventional production plan. It makes functional use of its dramatic material, the situations grow out of the theme and are controlled by it, rather than by some stereotyped notion of dramatic technique. The language is carefully adjusted to the characters and is not conceived as a piece of literature apart from the speaker. Only perhaps in the universality of the theme is the play weakened. The process of rehearsal and production is a highly specialized one. It has always had, of course, great fascination for the nonprofessional, and much of the attractiveness of *Joan of Lorraine* must be credited to Mr. Anderson's revelation of the life behind the curtain. But to illustrate one specialized problem by referring to another equally specialized is not to provide much illumination.

The purpose of the poet and of the playwright, and hence of the poetic dramatist, is to select details from the chaos of existence and arrange them into a pattern which can be comprehended by the spectator. The playwright's reward is the satisfaction of creation, of arrangement; the spectator's reward is to become a more conscious man. The playwright who cannot or will not attempt this illumination denies his art and cheats the spectator. Thus the true poet of the theater is not necessarily concerned in the least with the traditional forms and language of poetry, but with making all the elements at his disposal—plot, actor, action, stage, lighting, setting, music, speech—unite to serve as a vehicle for his theme, his vision, or his interpretation of man's fate. The American theater has produced its share of poetic dramas, not one of which is in debt to the conventions of poetic literature. *Roadside, Mourning Becomes Electra, Here Come the Clowns,* these are among the great achievements of the poetry of the theater where Everyman, as Yeats said, may see his own image.

6

AMERICAN COMEDY

WHEN the newly formed committee to determine the Pulitzer Prize Award for the best drama of the season met in 1918, their first selection was *Why Marry?*, a highly successful comedy by Jesse Lynch Williams. Although the comedy seems stilted today it is easy to see its appeal for the judges: Williams was a novelist and his work was more "literary" than most of his fellow playwrights; *Why Marry?* appears to be a play of manners, employing the tool of high wit rather than low humor for its comic ends. Its repartee is up-to-date, journalistically and morally. When the hero and the heroine decide to live together without benefit even of civil licence, the Judge who serves as commentator cries, "The strike against marriage. It was bound to come"; when the successful business man talks of the survival of the fittest, his brother asks, "The fittest for what?—for making money! The only kind of fitness encouraged to survive, to reproduce its species."

Marriage, the characters declare over and over again, is woman's only trade, and the audience is encouraged to watch critically the juxtaposition of a mating of the Old School—with the romantic juvenile trapped by the wiles of the girl he thinks he loves—and a mating of the New, in which two young scientists try to establish a relationship based on trust, mutual interests, and the rights of the individual. Thus far the action is an effective rewriting of a portion of Shaw's *Getting Married*. But Williams was unable to hold either the line of his action or his apparent moral. In the end his revolutionary couple, whom he has apparently been applauding for their determination, are legally married by a Pinerotic trick:

JUDGE. For the last time! before it's too late, Ernest! You know that in the eyes of God, you *are* taking this woman to be your wife.

ERNEST. In the eyes of *God*, I *do* take Helen to be my wife—but—

JUDGE. You, Helen! Speak, woman, speak!

HELEN. I take Ernest to be my husband in the eyes of God, but—

JUDGE. Then, since you, Ernest, and you, Helen, have made this solemn declaration before God and in the presence of witnesses, I, by the authority vested in me by the laws of this State, do now pronounce you man and wife!

The exclamation points scattered through the Judge's speeches are an accurate measure of the feverish temperature of his actions. Whatever point the play may have had, whatever purpose the wit may have served, point and wit are abandoned in the teeth of the final curtain. And the careful anonymity of the "State" whose authority is vested in the Judge suggests that the denouement is derived from that great casebook of legal fictions to which the playwright in difficulties can always turn.

Why Marry? is occasionally witty, fundamentally insincere, and no more American than the Shavian work from whence it comes. The comedy of manners with a few exceptions has never been typical of American playwrighting. *The New York Idea* stands apart, and some of the lighter works of Philip Barry *(Paris Bound, Holiday, The Animal Kingdom)* and S. N. Behrman *(The Second Man, Biography),* but the manners these plays reflect are neither American nor universal. They are the conventional manners of high comedy. The situations are remodelled from century-old stock and the characters would be reasonably comfortable in a Restoration chocolate house, a Parisian salon, or an Edwardian garden party.

Actually it is in another kind of comedy that the American theater has made its unique and most typical achievement. If critics tend to dismiss it as ephemeral, the records of the stage confute them with ample evidence of its durability, and historians of the drama with demonstrations of the legitimacy of its origins. The roots of this comedy are deep in the American character and customs and ways of looking at things.

Searching for a native dramatic tradition, John Dos Passos once wrote of the popular successes of the nineteenth century:

Already plays like *Blue Jeans* and *Uncle Tom's Cabin* and *Ben Hur* had a quality that distinguished them from their British equivalents. The series of ten-twenty-thirty melodramas and sob plays with their accompanying pie-slinging farces were a very genuine expression of the period of crude industrial expansion when people's energies were so drained by the physical effort of building up the country and their own fortunes that they had no need of safety valves.

Dos Passos praises the skill by which vaudeville performers "put themselves over individually to the audience" in the few moments allotted to their turns, and acknowledges the success of musical comedy and burlesque in achieving satire. In vaudeville, burlesque and musical comedy, he points out, is "the raw material for anything anyone wants to make."

These remarks were written as the Preface to John Howard Lawson's *Roger Bloomer* (see p. 99), but they have great validity as a preface to a consideration of the development of American comedy. A native form did arise out of the most popular elements of vaudeville and burlesque, and it was the comedians and music-hall performers who gave it birth, fostered its growth, and who still control its fortunes.

Historically American comedy began with Royall Tyler's *The Contrast* (1787), a pale reflection of *The School for Scandal* except for its one vital character, Jonathan, the Yankee. As a New Englander, Jonathan would never be confused with his realistically observed fellows in the plays of O'Neill. He is what we would today call a stereotype, a forerunner of a hundred vaudeville and radio comedians who specialize in racial caricature. He dances and sings "Yankee Doodle," talks Down-East slang and blunders with the Mother Tongue, but, as the popular song once declared, he gets there just the same. It is his ultimate success that distinguishes him from the comic stereotypes of British and Continental drama. They are satirized, mocked, and defeated; he is funny without being ridiculed. The machine-made melodramas that flooded the theater of the nineteenth century delighted to feature the "hick" who could outsmart the best that a more sophisticated society could bring against him. His almost inevitable victory was an expression of national optimism and self-confidence, and even historical figures like Davy Crockett (see p. 77) were remade in this image.

The minstrel show, as it developed from a concert into a variety performance, established the stage negro in a similar position, while many of the star performers in music halls based their turns on caricatures of the immigrants who had poured into the melting pot: Dutch, Irish, Italian, all bumbling in action and speech but ending always on top of their particular heap. Names will mean little in dealing with such evanescent material, but the farces of Charles Burke, the comic skits produced at Burton's Olympic, Hackett's Yankee Trader, and Chanfrau's dimly remembered Bowery B'hoy are elements in the tradition.

At the beginning of the present century, native comedy is best represented by the farces of Harrigan and Hart and of Weber and Fields. The adventures of the Mulligan Guards and of the tall thin Dutchman and the short fat Dutchman grow directly out of the slapdash action of the minstrel skit as the characters grow directly out of the stock types of burlesque. Here in the mockery of the serious, the classic, the formal, and the eventual victory of the much-beaten underdog is the theatrical equivalent of the tall talk and the comic folk story which reflect so accurately the American temper. Here, waiting for a playwright to put them to use, or give them form and purpose, were the elements of an American comedy.

One of the earliest to try his hand was Charles Hoyt in a series of musical farces, broadly satirizing such contemporary events as an election or the Temperance movement.

Hoyt was, however, more concerned with the speed and implausibility of his action than in justifying the ways of his caricatures to men. *A Trip to Chinatown* (1891), his most famous work, is also his most typical. There is a plot, of sorts, involving two young men and two eligible young ladies, a widow in search of a husband, a health faddist named Welland Strong, and minor characters named Slavin Payne and Noah Heap. The dialogue, which consists mainly of puns, is sufficient to get the actors on and off the stage, but since most of the action consists of racing through doors, nothing more is required of it. One hilarious scene, in a San Francisco restaurant, presents adjoining private rooms occupied by two parties, neither aware of the other's presence and avoiding discovery by hairtrigger-timed entrances and exits. As an added attraction the plot is interrupted at regular intervals by the introduction of songs, like "The Bowery" and "Reuben, Reuben," which have only the most tenuous connection with the situation or the characters. *A Trip to Chinatown* is a highly entertaining, breathlessly active farce. Hoyt's comic formula, and it has proved its usefulness many times since, was to demand as many doors as the set could reasonably support and to thrust his comic-strip figures in and out of them at maximum speed. The effect was not unlike that of a Mack Sennett comedy.

A step beyond Hoyt was taken by George Ade in declaring his intention of writing native comedies that would truthfully and amusingly *reveal* his fellow countrymen *without ridiculing* them. If some latitude is permitted the definition of "truthfully," Ade may properly be considered the first playwright of the New School of American comedy, combining rapid action, farcical situations, and a knack for indigenous character sketches. Like Hoyt, Ade began writ-

ing for the musical stage, and carried over many of its techniques into his legitimate comedies.

The County Chairman (1903), in fact, needs only a set
of lyrics to qualify as a musical comedy. The plot deals
with a contest for the political control of a small Midwest-
ern town in which one of the contestants is in love with
his rival's daughter. A ready-made chorus is at hand in the
villagers, and an opportunity for the required spectacle in
the outdoor meeting with its stump oratory, brass band,
banners and uniforms. The dialogue has in it much of the
technique of the variety show, described by Professor Quinn
as "planting the remark for the sake of the answer." Asks
the hero's rival, "We have got a clean majority of three
hundred, ain't we?" To which his manager replies, "You
got about three hundred. I don't know how *clean* it is."

There is gentle but legitimate spoofing of politics in the
lower echelons. The opening scene displays a cracker-barrel
Senate in full session in front of the village store. One
wiseacre is especially scornful of Washington's inaction over
the "Behrin' sea business" with Great Britain.

BRISCOE. As usual they're talkin' compromise and arbitration. Arbitration nothin'! We licked 'em twice an' as sure as
my name's Jefferson Briscoe, we'll have to do it again."
UNCLE ECK. Jeff, where is this Behrin' sea?

There is a pause, for Briscoe obviously has no notion, but
as the crowd begins to snigger, he blusters:

Don't make no difference where it is. The question is air we,
the greatest and most powerful nation on earth, goin' to set
back and be bully-ragged an' horn-swoggled by some Jim-Crow[1]

[1] i.e. "tricky" (*Dictionary of American Usage*).

island that looks, by ginger, like a freckle on the ocean! If they
had any backbone at Washington—

Ade assimilated in Briscoe a number of American comic
modes: the native lingo, the jingoism, the political assurance; all that he failed to do was cast him as hero. But such
a move was not long in coming.

Out of the variety houses and into the legitimate theater
came George M. Cohan, the apostle of rampant Americanism. With a sharp ear for the colloquial speech of New York
and the other cities he encountered in his professional
tours, with his single-minded devotion to the color combination in Old Glory, he created a wise-cracking, quick-
footed, dashing young hero who could instantaneously
declare and prove his superiority to all lesser mortals, "reu-
bens" or "limeys" or both. Heels clicking and all flags
unfurled, the Cohan hero sang and acted his way through
a series of patriotic fairy tales reflecting accurately and in
detail the optimism and self-confidence of Yankee-
Doodledom.

The Yankee Prince (1908) is typical. Here a group of
Chicagoans find themselves in England where they prove
their superiority by laughing at English customs, speech,
and manners. It is considered an excessively boisterous joke,
for instance, to call the unfortunate nobleman in the
plot, "Myrtle." And the contemporary audience would take
it as an expected compliment and not as a *tour de farce*
that the hero got to shake the hand of King Edward because
he bore a letter of introduction from "the greatest gentleman in the world"—John L. Sullivan. In Cohan's later
plays, such as *Get-Rich-Quick Wallingford* and *Broadway
Jones,* there is a tempering of the excesses, and at the end
of his career when he was billing himself as The American

Actor he was almost indulgent towards his youthful jingoism.

His contribution should not be minimized. The wise-crack is a peculiarly American form of speech, and Cohan takes full advantage of it. The older school of comedy had depended for much of its comic dialogue on the long, formal speech elaborating a whimsical idea; most celebrated in nineteenth-century comedy were such scenes as Lady Gay Spanker's description of a hunt in *London Assurance,* or the lengthy narratives of Lord Dundreary and company in *Our American Cousin,* all of which were cast into a language that was native only to the stage and called for careful development and leisurely appreciation. But Cohan, with his years of vaudeville behind him, knew the effectiveness of winning an audience with a phrase and convulsing it with a sentence. Consequently he wrote into his plays scenes, like those between Kid Burns and the natives of New Rochelle in *Forty-Five Minutes from Broadway,* which sound almost like the "cross fire and snappy patter" turns on the Keith Circuit. Brevity, he demonstrated, was the soul and body of the wisecrack, and the wisecrack was the heart of American comic dialogue.

Once the pattern was established there was no lack of skilled journeymen to put it to use. The affiliation between legitimate comedy and the vaudeville sketch is apparent in Winchell Smith's *The Fortune Hunter* (1909), of which Cohan was the coproducer. Smith bases his plot on the efforts of a young man-about-the-city to make good in a country town. Wangling a job in a drug store, he pretends to be a knowing mixer of sodas; when a customer demands one, he first tries to mix it like a highball, then misuses the fountain spigot and soaks himself and the customer. The use of water, or a seltzer bottle, as a weapon is one of the basic "gags" of low comedy and the burlesque show. Yet Smith manages to keep his hero sympathetic and likable regardless of his farcical misadventures.

Some of the other characters are not so completely legitimatized. The villain, the local banker and president of the temperance league, is given a nervous habit, an involuntary wink, out of which Smith manufactures some broad comic business. Meeting the hero in the drug store, he asks for a drink of soda water.

NAT: Would you like vanilla?
LOCKWOOD: No, just soda. *(For the first time Nat sees the wink from Lockwood's affected eye)*
NAT: I beg your pardon.
LOCKWOOD: I say, just plain —*(Winking again)* soda.
NAT: On the level?
LOCKWOOD: What? *(Winks again)*
NAT: I understand. *(Gets whiskey bottle, turns out drink, and fills it with soda)*
LOCKWOOD: *(Drinking, smacking his lips, etc.)* How can anyone want intoxicating liquors when they can get such a bracin' drink as this?

All is, of course, not farcical action in *The Fortune Hunter*. Ned's purpose in coming from New York was to win a bet that he can marry a village heiress inside of a year. Coming for troth, he remains to praise the country virtues of honesty, hard work, and churchgoing, thus providing a moral not to say sentimental color to the comedy. But while using moral commonplaces to create sympathy for his hero, the playwright does not forget that his business is comedy. After the hero has recognized his own hypocrisy and firmly resolved on reformation, he proposes to the heroine in her dooryard with these solemn and heartfelt words: "I love you, Betty, and I want to be a man. Won't you forgive me

and be my wife?" At this moment a downpour of rain
commences, and Betty accepts him. Unmindful of the rain
the lovers embrace, and the girl's father appears with an
umbrella which he holds over them as the curtain falls.

The Fortune Hunter with its mingling of farce and sentiment is typical of the new comedy, which makes free use
of both modes without allowing either to dominate the
play. Even such apparent satire as *It Pays to Advertise*
(1914) by Roi Cooper Megrue and Walter Hackett, in
which a man is forced to live up to his advertising, is in
essence a bustling combination of romance and slapstick. It
is perhaps satirical to point out, as the play does, that hen's
eggs are widely consumed where duck eggs are discarded
because the hen makes no bones about announcing the
availability of her product. But romantic love and paternal
love intrude upon the satire, and the point of the wit is
frequently lost in the slamming of doors with which each
setting is generously supplied.

The next development of the comic tradition may be
credited to George Kelly. Having served his apprenticeship
in vaudeville, Kelly came to the legitimate theater in 1922
with *The Torchbearers,* a farcical treatment of the preten-
sions of amateur actors. Three acts of pure slapstick, written
with the professional's distaste for those who treat his profession as a pastime, ridicule the members of a little theater
group who cannot remember lines, or keep out of each
other's way, or cross the stage without tripping. The central figure, Mrs. J. Duro Pampinelli, as leader of the group
is treated not with ridicule or distaste, but downright
venom. Her vanity, her shallow artiness, her inhumanity,
and her willingness to victimize her credulous actors are
vigorously exposed. Since Mrs. Pampinelli is a special type
who appears infrequently on the American scene, it can

only be supposed that Kelly was working off a personal grudge. At any rate, the lack of sympathy in his portrait of her is in marked contrast with his portrait of Aubrey Piper.

Aubrey is the hero of *The Show-Off* (1924), a type who can be found in every other American family and one universally disliked. Actually a clerk in the freight office of the Pennsylvania Railroad, he pretends to have eighty men under him. Actually an unwelcome guest in the Fisher home, he brazenly introduces himself to a stranger as the head of the house. With his irritating whinny, his tasteless jokes, his backslapping and braggadocio, he is the apotheosis of the common pest summed up in the title of his play. One action after another—as he imposes himself on the Fishers, turns the unmarried daughter against her mother, fixes himself like a parasite on the son-in-law, interferes with the son's business affairs—each is calculated to turn the audience against him. Yet Kelly, in the tradition of Ade and Cohan and Smith, and more honestly than any of his predecessors, presents his comic hero truthfully, without ridicule or spite.

He calls his play "A Transcript of Life in Three Acts," and he employs the devices of the realistic theater to represent middle-class suburban life with utmost fidelity. In setting, characterization, and speech he is minutely faithful to his chosen milieu. Not only the diction but the very rhythms of his dialogue reflect the bourgeois society as accurately as the matters under discussion: marriage, and death, and making both ends meet. Aubrey, with a carnation always in his buttonhole, moves through this world without surrendering to it. He believes in the success stories of *The American Magazine* and in the moral principle of time payments. His jokes drive placid Mr. Fisher from his own home; his wooing of Amy Fisher causes amply-told

anguish; he borrows a friend's car, breaks a traffic regulation, runs into a streetcar, breaks the arm of a policeman
and naïvely announces that he has neglected to renew his
driver's licence. His answer to the consequences of each
action is unabashed: anger produces more bad but completely good-humored jokes, sharp words produce philosophical clichés, and arrest brings a frontal attack on the
inefficiency of the police department.

Yet with great dramatic skill Kelly manages to leave us
with sympathy, even affection, for Aubrey. This is not
achieved by sentimentalizing him; Aubrey ends the play as
he began it, bad jokes, loud mouth and all. Even during
the pathetic scene in which Mr. Fisher's death is announced,
Aubrey is relentlessly himself. His wife suggests that, since in
the confusion he has had no food, she will prepare something for him. He instantly dramatizes the situation, both
in speech and action:

> It'll all be the same at the finish,—whether I've had my dinner
> or not. (*He rests his fist on the table, throws his head back,
> and looks to the stars*) "Sic transit gloria mundi." And we
> never get used to it. (*He moves across to the upper right corner
> of the center table*) The paths of glory lead but to the grave.
> (*He stops again, leans on the table and looks out and away off*)
> And yet we go on,—building up big fortunes—only to leave
> them to the generations yet unborn. Well, (*He moves forward
> to the chair at the right*)—so it goes. (*He sits down, throws one
> leg across his knee, and shakes his head up and down slowly*)
> And so it will *always* go, I suppose. "Sic transit gloria mundi."

Aubrey is a play actor, always slightly out of the situation.

No, Aubrey does not change; it is our attitude towards
him that is changed. If we grit our teeth at his early appear-
ances, we soon smile, and eventually learn to pity him.
From the first, of course, Amy has been on his side, for she

loves him. Then, after the father's death, the married daughter begins to perceive a virtue in him: "He does his best. He works every day, and he gives her his money; and nobody ever heard of him looking at another woman." The son-in-law, too, tolerates him and even supports him because of the genuineness of his love for Amy. Several scenes of the play reveal the sincerity of his love, and the son-in-law is enough of a man-of-the-world to recognize the rarity and value of such honest devotion.

This change in the attitude of the spectator towards Aubrey might lead to an almost sentimental conclusion, were it not for Kelly's determination to maintain the comic mode. The sister declares: "I feel kind of sorry for him sometimes. He'd so love to be important; and, of course, he never will be." But before we can experience this sense of pity too deeply, Aubrey commits his brashest act. Amy's young brother has discovered a formula to prevent the rusting of metals and is about to sell it to a corporation for $50,000. Unknown to the family, Aubrey visits the company and demands double the sum, representing himself as head of the family and "connected with" the Pennsylvania Railroad. The mother sourly remarks, "It's too bad they didn't know what you do down there; and call your bluff." Aubrey's reply is perfectly honest: "I beat them to it; I called theirs first."

The ending, the triumph of Aubrey Piper, is more than a farcical twist, more than a comic reward for the comic hero, more than irony. Aubrey's explanation for the capitulation of the company broadens the theme of the play to include a whole facet of American culture. *The Show-Off* embraces all whose creed used to be found in success stories of *The American Magazine;* not just Aubrey, but big business is compounded of bluff, and theatricality, and bragging, and the mouthing of sententious proverbs. The audience will understand Mrs. Fisher's groan as the final curtain arrives with The Show-Off as cock of the walk, but it will admire and perhaps even like Aubrey for putting to good use that talent which it is death to hide.

None of Kelly's later works quite comes up to this comic masterpiece. In *Daisy Mayme* (1926) he again drew a life-like picture of a grubby suburban society whose small conventions are breached by an individualist. But the majority of his later works, *Craig's Wife, Behold the Bridegroom* (see p. 49) are serious, even didactic, studies of women in and out of love. The comic element and the objectivity of *The Show-Off* are increasingly submerged.

The native comic tradition was nevertheless very much alive. Its vitality is attested by the records of a series of plays extending across the twenties and thirties and forties and connected with the names of George S. Kaufman, Edna Ferber, Moss Hart, Morrie Ryskind, Marc Connelly, and George Abbott. Of these the most important are Kaufman and Abbott, the first as playwright and play doctor, the second as producer of plays in which the formula of burlesque-*cum*-vaudeville-*cum*-sentimentality is thoroughly exploited.

Kaufman is properly recognized as the great collaborator since he has done most of his work as a partner of Hart, Ferber, Ryskind, and Connelly. His plays are in many modes—sometimes sentimental, sometimes broadly satirical, sometimes simply comic, depending apparently on his collaborator of the moment. But Kaufman's own contribution seems to be relatively fixed; the three elements that all these collaborations share are: Kaufman, a peculiar type of comic hero, and the wisecrack unlimited.

Kaufman's comic hero is not merely, as in the tradition, an apparently naïve fellow whose good sense and sound moral character help him to outwit his more sophisticated or experienced opponents. Instead of the Ade-Cohan-Smith type, he is presented as downright stupid, winning his way to success only because the peculiar world through which he moves shifts its values and principles of action with disconcerting, or gratifying, ease. The characterization reaches its apex, or nadir, in George, the comic hero of *Once in a Lifetime* (1930). Intended as a satire on the making of movies the play might almost be read as the *reductio ad absurdum* of that American sentimental cliché, the little man.

George is the "feeder" in a vaudeville act, the man whose stupid questions are an excuse for his partners' smart answers. When the other members of the team decide to take advantage of the invention of the "talkies" and go to Hollywood, George stumbles along. Once there he insults the studio owner and is made a director for his "honesty." He works from the wrong script, forgets to turn on the lights, and absent-mindedly cracks nuts throughout the shooting. The resulting film tells, in almost total darkness, a story no longer in the current vogue to the accompaniment of unidentifiable thumping noises. The film is greeted as an artistic triumph, and at the end of the play it is apparent that George is the new wonder boy of the movies. He thus becomes the little man *in excelsis,* and his career is a parody of the success story.

Much of the dialogue in *Once in a Lifetime* depends for its humor and point upon the form of the wisecrack, at which Kaufman is an absolute genius. Unlike the epigram, the wisecrack does not depend solely upon succinctness of diction, clever parallelism, or inversion of the expected. The wisecrack is more dependent for its effect upon timing or word order, sometimes in utter defiance of grammar and syntax. In the opening scene of *Once in a Lifetime* the female member of the vaudeville team is worried because their leader, Jerry, has not managed to obtain bookings:

MAY. *(Nervously)* What's Jerry up to, George? Is he going to land us something or isn't he? How much longer are we going to lay around here?

GEORGE. Don't ask me—ask Jerry.

MAY. I'm gonna—and we'll have a showdown tonight. The Automat don't spell home to me.

GEORGE. *(Just a literal boy)* We don't live there.

MAY. We do everything but sleep there, and we'd be doing that if they could get beds into them slots.

A few moments later:

MAY. The question is: What do we do about bookings? Are we going to crash the big time or aren't we?

GEORGE. We were doing all right on the small time. We could be working right along—you know what the Booking Office told us.

MAY. And you know where the Booking Office books us. Bellows Falls, Vermont.

GEORGE. I liked it there.

MAY. What?

GEORGE. We had a good dinner there. With jello.

To substitute *those* for *them* in the concluding speech of the first passage, or to alter the punctuation which guides the timing in the third and sixth speeches of the second passage, would be to destroy their comic effect, for the very sound of the spoken phrase is an important ingredient in the successful wisecrack.

Characteristic, also, of Kaufman's comedy is his knack of arriving at the apposite visual gag to emphasize his satiric point. *June Moon* (1929), written with Ring Lardner, is a broad burlesque of the manners and morals of Tin Pan Alley. When a successful composer comes upon the window washer of his office building picking out an "original" tune on the office piano, he does the appropriate thing: seizing the brush and squeegee, he commences to wash the window. The President, in *Of Thee I Sing*, is saved from impeachment when his wife dances into the Senate and announces that he is about to become a father.

Of Thee I Sing (1931), written in collaboration with Morrie Ryskind and set to music by George Gershwin, is the masterpiece of comedy in the native tradition used for satirical purposes. Actually a highly cynical view of national politics, it describes the campaign of John P. Wintergreen whose successful platform is nothing more than "Put Love in the White House." Beginning with the expected singing and dancing of musical comedy, it presents a comic interpretation of political corruption. Wintergreen, an ignorant opportunist, a liar and a fraud, escapes from all the traps his opponents set for him, wins Mary Turner and the election. The whole cynicism of the work is summed up in the title of its theme song, "Of Thee I Sing, *Baby*."

In a kind of subplot, the play tells of the adventures of Alexander Throttlebottom, the typical Kaufman comic hero, who is hoodwinked into running for vice president, is elected and comes perilously close to the presidency itself during the impeachment proceedings against Wintergreen. A brief scene from early in his career will illustrate the nature of the comic hero, the careful timing of the comic dialogue (that is, the nature of the wisecrack), and the broadness of the satire. The place is a smoke-filled room during a national convention. The delegates have just decided that Wintergreen is their party's choice.

FULTON. The people of this country demand John P. Wintergreen for president, and they're going to get him whether they like it or not. And between you and me, gentlemen, I don't think they like it. *(There is a knock at the door)* Come in.

THROTTLEBOTTOM. *(Entering)* Hi, gentlemen!

FULTON. Yes, sir. What can we do for you?

THROTTLEBOTTOM. *(All smiles)* Hello, Mr. Fulton.

FULTON. I'm afraid I don't quite place you. Your face is familiar but—

THROTTLEBOTTOM. I'm Throttlebottom.

FULTON. What?

THROTTLEBOTTOM. Alexander Throttlebottom.

JONES. *(Pushing him right out)* We're very busy, my good man. If you'll just—

THROTTLEBOTTOM. But I'm Throttlebottom.

FULTON. I understand, Mr. Teitelbaum, but just at present—

GILHOOLEY. You come back later on.

LIPMAN. After we're gone.

THROTTLEBOTTOM. *(Insistent about it)* But I'm Throttlebottom. I'm the candidate for vice-president.

FULTON. That's the fellow!

GILHOOLEY. Of course!

FULTON. What's your name again?

THROTTLEBOTTOM. Alexander—

FULTON. Of course! I nominated you! Alexander! Boys, this is—What's your first name, Mr. Alexander?

THROTTLEBOTTOM. That's my first name, Alexander.

FULTON. Well, well. Alexander Alexander.

GILHOOLEY. Well, that certainly is a coincidence. *(A Waiter has arrived with room service. Check in hand, he looks uncertainly around for the victim)*

THROTTLEBOTTOM. But that isn't my last name. It's Throttlebottom.

LIPMAN. Throttle what?

THROTTLEBOTTOM. Bottom.

LIPMAN. How do you spell it?

THROTTLEBOTTOM. *(As he starts to spell Lipman takes the check from the Waiter and writes)* 'T-h-r-o-t-t-l-e-b-o-t-t-o-m.'

LIPMAN. Right! And thank you very much.

(The Waiter goes, and with him the signed check)
FULTON. Well, sir, we're very glad indeed to see you, and very
proud to have you on our ticket. Sit down.
(They all sit, leaving no place for Throttlebottom)

Such a scene is typical of the comedy in which Kaufman
was involved at its best: broad, vigorous, and timed to the
last syllable.

In the middle of the nineteen-thirties a singular group
of comedies had extraordinary success both in New York
and on the road. Although they were written by various
authors, the mark of George Abbott as producer or director
is so deeply impressed on them that they are properly referred to as the Abbott comedies.

Abbott brought nothing new to the American theater.
His work was rather an intensification—refinement is hardly
the word—of the tradition. His little man is just a shade
smaller, the tempo of his action a shade faster, his unexpected curtain a shade more fortuitous. J. C. Holm's *Three
Men on a Horse,* which opened the series in 1935, chose
as its hero a lyric writer for a greeting card company who
becomes preposterously involved with a race-track betting
syndicate. *Boy Meets Girl* (1935), by Bella and Samuel
Spewack, is Abbott's contribution to Hollywood satire, and
makes an interesting comparison with Kaufman's *Once in
a Lifetime.* Kaufman's hero was a vaudevillian; the
Spewacks move farther on the spectrum of stupidity to
relate the adventures of a surpassingly naïve waitress who
becomes the unmarried mother of a child prodigy. *Room
Service* (1937), by Murray and Boretz, is a frenetic document describing the attempts of a shoestring producer to
stage a play, the little man being the unsophisticated
playwright.

Having exhausted the possibilities of adult stupidity,
Abbott turned to two plays about adolescents, *Brother Rat*

(1937) by Monks and Finkelhoffe, and *What a Life!* (1938), by Clifford Goldsmith. The first describes the behavior of cadets in a military prep school, the second the frenzied life of a high school student, Henry Aldrich, who has since become almost a national hero. In both plays the authors capitalize on the supposed tendency of the adolescent to go to any lengths of ingenuity to escape the consequences of some simple situation. The action is fast and furious and, generally, fantastic, accompanied by banging doors, exits through windows, and more hiding in closets and under beds than the theater had seen since the Restoration. Satire and sentiment are minimized; the amusement lies in the speed of the action, the staccato dialogue, and the slightly sadistic complications through which the hero must squirm to eventual victory.

It is perhaps difficult for Americans to recognize the highly individual character of the American comic tradition; it has dominated our stage for so many years and reflects so precisely the tempo of our daily life that it may be taken for granted. Here, however, is the description of a comedy of the Abbott type as seen by an English critic, J. T. Grein:

[The actors] work with a will and like Trojans; they rush about the stage as if panic had stricken them; they blurt out their wild bits of dialogue as if under pneumatic pressure; they shout, gesticulate, play tricks, gambol with the irresponsible *abandon* of an amiable lunatic asylum let loose; they give us no time to think, to analyze or to criticize; somehow they laugh and will make us respond—and the result is that people on the stage and people in the house let themselves gayly go, both parties really full well aware that they are "dashed" if they know what it is all about.[1]

[1] Quoted in M. J. Moses, *Representative American Dramas,* Boston, 1941. p. 331.

Mr. Grein happens to be describing *A Pair of Sixes,* a comedy of World War I vintage. That he might well be referring to a performance of *Brother Rat* or *What a Life!* indicates the length and breadth of the American comic tradition as it spans fifty years of theatrical history. Nor is it, because half a hundred years old, declining into senescence. It shows no signs of aging. Ruth Gordon's *Over Twenty-One* (1944), a satire on officers' training during the recent war, makes as great use of mechanical effects for comic purposes as do such famous vaudeville turns as "The Plasterers" (Willy, West, and McGinty). *Born Yesterday* (1946), by Garson Kanin, is distantly related to the myth of Pygmalion and Galatea. Only, in this Americanized instance, Galatea is made over from a chorus girl into a liberal-intellectual smart enough to thwart the villainous machinations of her former lover, and Pygmalion, as a reporter for the *New Republic,* becomes the triumphant little man, with liberal overtones. Finally, Mr. Grein's words could surely be applied to *Mister Roberts* (1948), by Thomas Heggen and Joshua Logan, the great comedy success at the turn of the half-century. Indeed its picture of life on a naval supply vessel in the South Pacific was described as "Brother Rat gone to sea." The sailors are straight from the Abbott school of comedy, and the hero, a lieutenant who longs for action, differs from the other little men only in being permitted a modicum of intelligence and a sentimentalized end.

The question naturally arises whether these plays are anything more than American. Comedy is always suspect of being subliterary, and the combination of farce and sentimentality, the glorification of the worm-who-turns, is frequently productive of nothing but ephemeral entertainment. From the length of their original runs, and from the frequency of their revival, it is apparent that there is something in the form, the tempo, and the attitude of these comedies that is peculiarly attractive to an American audience. And in the case of such plays as *The Show-Off, Of Thee I Sing,* and *Born Yesterday,* the native comic style has produced notable satire and comic portraiture. With vigorous good humor it has sported with our national follies, and if its conclusions have been on the side of optimism, the stage as always is but echoing back the public voice.

7

ACT DROP, 1951

W
HEN the last curtains fell on Broadway
on the night of May 31, 1951, the audiences departed with
no sense that they were participating in an historical action.
That fifty seasons of American drama had been completed
in this century was of considerably less significance to them
than the quality of the entertainment they had just witnessed or the difficulty of catching the last train to Con-
necticut. Probably the experiencing of a work of art should
not include such extra-aesthetic or historical considerations
except in the inevitable retrospect, yet it is true that much
of the quality of their entertainment was a product of the
changes and chances of the fifty preceding seasons.

The fact that a large portion of the audience was com-
muters or transient visitors to the metropolis indicates one

stable factor in the half-century. New York was still the theatrical center of the country. More than ever, producers aimed at success on Broadway and were less and less interested in the rest of America. The Road had disintegrated into a kind of unimproved, farm-to-market byway connecting New York with the two or three cities where plays might be tested on live audiences. An occasional great success might venture west of Buffalo after its Broadway run was completed, or a famous star might dare appear in the vast city auditoriums or college theaters that had replaced opera houses in the rest of the country. But for the most part, Broadway producers were content to sell their successful properties to the movies to tour the country in cans instead of on increasingly expensive Pullmans.

Obviously the changes of fifty years are more noticeable than the constants, and the most obvious change is the proliferating costs of production. More than most professions, the theater has always been a gamble, but in the old days it was a gamble shared by all. Actors, stage hands and author gambled on being paid; the producer gambled on getting his money back through success at the box office. It did not much matter to many producers whether their success was the result of public approval and patronage or their own astuteness in absconding with the receipts while the actors were hard at work. The unionization of the theatrical professions put a stop to such exploitation of labor and exercised a salutary control over some of the more nimble "showmen." But, designed to correct an extreme condition, unionization became itself extreme and imposed certain inhibitions on production which have not been altogether healthy for the American theater.

The present cost of raising the curtain on a single-set small cast show averages about $50,000. For a musical, the pre-opening cost may run as high as $300,000. Twenty years ago a play that attained 100 performances was officially considered a success. Now, the producer calculates in terms of a full season's run. In the average Broadway theater accommodating straight plays and seating say 900 people eight performances a week for forty weeks, the play must attract a quarter of a million theatergoers before it can be considered to have been a safe investment. This is an appalling burden to place upon any work of art, a pre posterous demand to make of a playwright.

The appeal to reason, however, will not breach the out· works of the economic problem. It exists, persists, and grows more serious with every production. The mere survival of the theater as anything more than a commercial peep show is surprising in the face of it; the high quality of even a handful of plays in a given season a miracle. Here. of course, the psychology of the play*goer* enters in. For some people attendance at the theater is a gala occasion, the proper celebration of an anniversary or of a stroke of good luck; or it is a means to develop social or commercial goodwill. These playgoers supply the vast audiences that keep musicals running for two or three seasons, and they sometimes spill over into plays that have survived long enough to penetrate their preoccupations. But the audience that forms the nucleus on which the theater depends is a far different matter. Its reasons for playgoing are diverse: it goes for glamor, or escape; it is performing a ritual; it seeks understanding, affirmation, reconciliation. Playgoing is for it a habit, a mania, and sometimes a *raison d'être.*

Unlike most other aesthetic experiences, drama cannot be had cheaply or at second hand. Reading a play is as unsatisfactory as reading a musical score; a recorded or broadcast version is only half a play, being without the action;

and a televised or screened play is inevitably a distortion. So, in spite of all the obstacles that the theater can erect— high prices (plus the extortion money demanded by the parasitical ticket scalpers), uncomfortable seats, poor acoustics, and a general atmosphere intended to make the customer feel that his presence is being barely tolerated in a bordello reserved for some higher caste—in spite of these obstacles, playgoers persist in playgoing; because of this persistence, the American theater manages to produce as many good plays as any generation has a right to expect.

It is certainly true that the high cost and the difficulties of playgoing have honed our critical faculties to a razor-edge. Anything less than absolute perfection—whatever that may be—is apt to raise a frenzied hue and cry among the professional critics as if the producer had committed some kind of public nuisance, and to awaken sometimes vague and sometimes positive feelings of discontent among the ticket buyers. With the statistics for 1900 in mind, it is interesting to make a comparison with the 1950-51 season. Between September 1950 and June 1951, forty-three new plays were presented on Broadway. (There were also fourteen musical productions and thirty revivals both dramatic and musical.) Of these, nine either were or promised to be commercially successful. More important, of the total number, thirteen might fairly be considered as having something more than commercial success to their credit: freshness, experimentation, literacy, appositeness, craftsmanship.[1]

---

[1] Not to be mysterious, the plays referred to are: *The Country Girl,* Clifford Odets; *Darkness at Noon,* Sydney Kingsley; *The Rose Tattoo,* Tennessee Williams; *Second Threshold,* Philip Barry; *Billy Budd,* Louis Coxe and Robert Chapman; *The Autumn Garden,* Lillian Hellman; *Angel in the Pawnshop,* A. B. Schiffrin; *The Tower Beyond Tragedy,* Robinson Jeffers; *Stalag 17,* Bevan and Trzcinski; *Burning Bright,* John Steinbeck; *The Little Blue Light,* Edmund Wilson; *Borned in Texas,* Lynn Riggs. To these might

Statistics must not be relied upon in forming critical judgments or the historian might be tempted to draw up comparative tables of the estimated number of plays produced and those which might be considered successes in anything more than a commercial sense in all the great periods of theatrical production.

Certainly the "Americanness" of the Broadway theater is an established fact. Of the forty-three new plays, only eleven were imported, seven from England (one was successful), and one each from France, Spain, Ireland, and Canada (none was successful). But Americanism goes deeper than the mere country of origin of playwrights. To an astonishing and sometimes disturbing degree our drama is reflecting certain aspects of our nature that our other popular public arts have chosen to ignore.

It is clear from the offerings of the Broadway stage that the age of George M. Cohan is dead. To theatergoers this is somewhat less than an astonishing revelation. The age, in fact, predeceased Cohan. But in the so-called comic strips and magazines, one American can still lick three times his weight in wily Orientals or bullheaded Slavs; Superman is the typical American boy. The columnists of many of our popular journals continue to practice the art of wing-flapping and screaming like an eagle. Hollywood's wartime cycles dutifully put all the undrafted heroes through their Yankee Doodle paces. Yet the theater, during World War II, when it got down to timely subjects, concerned itself with the individuals who were forced to live under unfamiliar pressures. Indeed, one of the few genuine pieces of jingoism sang the untempered praises of our then ally, in

---

be added the revivals of *Twentieth Century*, *The Green Pastures*, *An Enemy of the People* (adapted by Arthur Miller), *The Royal Family*, *Idiot's Delight*, and *Night Music*.

Clifford Odets' adaptation of *The Russian People*. In rejecting both the romantic view of war as represented by the nineteenth-century *Shenandoah*, or the cynical view represented by the twentieth-century *What Price Glory?* the drama was reflecting the concern of most Americans to whom the war was an unpleasant necessity. Major Saranoff went to Hollywood to act out celluloid dreams of heroism for our idle or despondent hours; but Captain Blunschli was readily recognized by theatergoers as representing the truthful relationship between arms and the man.

Few plays of the 1950-51 season might be described as cynical or disillusioned. Sydney Kingsley's dramatization of the Koestler novel, *Darkness at Noon*, reflects the author's bitter discovery that the blood upon ideological hands is still human blood. Cynicism, like smug certainty, is an attitude of the immature. There are indications of maturity.

As one of the most successful of American playwrights, Lillian Hellman has stood her ground so firmly that she has often been accused of writing melodramas, plays in which her convictions of what was right battled openly— if unsuccessfully—with her convictions of what was wrong. Her most recent play, *The Autumn Garden*, returns to her favorite setting, the South, and to her favorite characters, the rich.

But *The Autumn Garden* is a broader and deeper view of her society and generation than any Miss Hellman has taken heretofore. In it she assembles a dozen characters in a summer resort on the Gulf of Mexico, characters who are for the most part hopelessly romantic. Year after year they have returned to the same boarding house, which becomes almost a symbol of their retreat from reality. For the proprietress it is her heritage, the one thing she was able to rescue from the wreckage of her father's estate, but to them all it is the past, elegant in its outlines, and worn shabby with the passing years. Against these characters and into this house Miss Hellman projects a sober and very mature young French girl whose struggles to play her assigned role in the romantic drama the others have chosen to enact are by turns funny, pathetic, and shockingly pointed. Beside her wisdom the other characters, whose lives have reached the sere and yellow of autumn, are mere babes in the wood. And the action of the play is contrived to bring each of these deluded romantics to a moment of perception, to a moment when his eyes are opened to his precise situation. But it is only a moment, for the dream closes in and life continues according to the demanded pattern.

In a number of ways this is Miss Hellman's most original play. Structurally, it escapes from the technical slickness which has been by turns the wonder and despair of her critics. Thematically, it avoids the black and white values that have controlled the action of her earlier plays. Humanely, it reveals the nature of our life, of our means of grace. *The Autumn Garden* does not state a thesis and draw up the battle lines. Instead it assembles a group of people, in nondescript uniforms, and allows them to play off against one other for three acts. There is plenty of action, of conflict, but the characters are never knocked down. They are only bumped a bit, so that they lose balance momentarily, and turn another side to the audience. Thus the play presents an almost Chekhovian image of society, never denying the chaos through which we move, but by the subtlest shaping and selection creating an order within the chaos and lending meaning to experience. Were it not utter foolishness to call so experienced a talent as Miss Hellman's promising, it would be proper to say that *The Au-*

tumn Garden was the most promising play of the year.

In sharp contrast to the tolerance and sympathy of Miss Hellman's play, the season produced Arthur Miller's adaptation of Ibsen's *An Enemy of the People*. In the Preface to the published text, Miller explains his laudable ambition to present Ibsen in "actable" English. He also defends certain omissions on the grounds that they make Ibsen sound like a fascist, which he could never be. In such matters Miller's grounds are as sure as anyone's: Ibsen was notoriously uncritical of scientific ideas, but certainly the general tendency of his works is in direct opposition to the tyranny of fascist philosophy.

What is most striking is the renovated hero who emerges in Miller's adaptation. Ibsen may have begun Dr. Stockmann as a self-portrait; the play is supposed to have been conceived in anger at the misunderstanding of *Ghosts*. But Stockmann as completed is in many ways the most human of Ibsen's characters. He is angry, forthright, radical. He has no patience with the materialism and shortsightedness of his fellows. In his immediate situation, he is also right. Yet he does not emerge in Ibsen's play as a Christlike reformer, a martyr to the community. He is as pigheaded scientifically as his brother is politically. His idealism is as shortsighted as the materialism of his opponents. Miller keeps some of Stockmann's attractive gusto, his fussiness and his forgetfulness. But he leaves out Stockmann's—and what is more important, Ibsen's—sense of humor.

In Ibsen's third act, in the editorial offices of the *People's Messenger*, Mayor Stockmann is hiding from his brother. Dr. Stockmann however discovers the mayor's hat and staff of office. In a moment of expansive self-confidence he puts on the hat and roots out his brother to poke fun at him. In Miller's version, Stockmann says to the Mayor; "I just wanted you to realize, Peter, that anyone may wear this hat in a democracy, and that a free citizen is not afraid to touch it."

Ibsen's final act takes place in Stockmann's house the day after he has been declared an enemy of the people in a public meeting. The doctor's reaction is magnificent and typical. Throughout the act he improvises, driving out the opportunists who would capitalize on his position, developing an increasing scorn for the power of the mob to harm him (he points out that they have not the courage to throw *big* stones at him, only gravel), and finally making a "great discovery:"

MRS. STOCKMANN. *(Half-despairing, half-admiring)* Another one?
DR. STOCKMANN. Yes. It is this, let me tell you—that the strongest man in the world is he who stands most alone.
MRS. STOCKMANN. *(Smiling and shaking her head)* Oh Thomas, Thomas!

Upon which a highly ambiguous curtain falls. Stockmann is without work, without patients, without money. He proposes to stay in the town, to support his family, to start a school. His wife is surely entitled to her combination of hopelessness and admiration.

But not in Miller's version. The reformer, the outspoken defender of the unpopular position, can no longer be treated as a comic figure. Stockmann picks up the rocks to preserve as "sacred relics," but without alluding to their size. The implication is that they represent the strength of the opposition. And at the end of the act, with the angry mob raging outside, the flickering light of their torches cast into the darkened room, Stockmann and his family cower in a corner far from the window. Mrs. Stockmann's line differs significantly from the original and so, even more significantly, does her husband's reply:

MRS. STOCKMANN. What's going to happen? Tom! What's going to happen?
DR. STOCKMANN. (. . . *with a trembling mixture of trepidation and courageous insistence*) I don't know. But remember now, everybody. You are fighting for the truth and that's why you're alone. And that makes you strong. We're the strongest people in the world . . . and the strong must learn to be lonely!

Most adaptations of the classics are watered versions. Miller's Ibsen might be more accurately described as evaporated. The essence of the play has been kept, perhaps magnified, but some of the humanity has been removed. For the man of Miller's generation, who reached maturity during the thirties, it is not possible to see the other side of the mountain. And if the mountain will not come to Mahomet, the prophet will hold his ground. In one sense, this represents the return to the absolute standards of melodrama, the defined good versus the defined evil, the oversimplification of values. In another sense, this is a precise mirror of an aspect of American culture at mid-century.

If Miller is approaching the techniques of a highly literate and serious melodrama, two new playwrights, Robert Chapman and Louis Coxe, might be said to approach the techniques of the ancient form of the morality play. In their dramatization of Herman Melville's short novel, *Billy Budd,* they seem to have resurrected the character of Everyman, the interested bystander in an allegorical conflict between the Virtues and the Vices. Since the modern tolerance for allegory has reached the point of no returns, they have cloaked it with more of the appearance of humanity than was the ancient custom. But since neither psychological nor economic determinism will satisfactorily explain the behavior of the characters or the tendency of the action, the spectator is forced to conclude that he is beholding the confrontation of Good and Evil and a demonstration that compromise must be affected for mere survival.

Admittedly this is a somewhat controversial interpretation of the original work. It has been suggested that Melville was not commending Captain Vere, but criticizing him for upholding the letter rather than the spirit of the law. Indeed it is significant of the national temper that when Vere swayed the decision of the court martial by his plea that the law must be upheld, members of the audience regularly protested aloud.

Whatever the validity of the interpretation, Coxe and Chapman have created an impressive dramatic work. *Billy Budd* is a short novel, but it is typically Melvillean in its sprawling form, with its untidy pursuit of the idea along any byway that presents itself. Such a structure is unproductive of effect in the theater, and the adaptors have wisely concentrated on creating a confined world and a controlling time for their action. The scene is a ship at sea, the time, after a mutiny during a war. A man-of-war is a community where the rules must be strictly followed, and in time of war—as we have too often discovered—the democratic tolerance for double or triple standards is replaced by the necessity of conforming. Thus the dramatists have reduced the universal conflict in *Billy Budd* to a microcosmic setting and action which may be comprehended and related to the disordered experiences of living.

The dramatization is not without flaws. Originally conceived as a verse play and later reworked as prose, some vestiges of the original form remain. Much of the effectiveness of the play depends upon the relations between men, sailor and sailor, sailor and officer, officer and officer: a kind of historical naturalism. But there are moments where the original verse still intrudes, where one character or another narrows his eyes, looks out over the footlights and utters gnomic lines about the sea, or life.

At such points it is again evident that modern playwrights have not learned to adjust themselves to the modern drama. Since many of them began their writing careers as poets they are reluctant to give up the special advantages of the poet in becoming dramatists. They are unwilling to recognize the total unsuitability of lyric expression in the realistic theater, and, more important, they are unwilling to grant that certain devices of the realistic theater serve precisely the function of poetic speech without a breech of illusion or of the unity of the play. A century ago Ibsen demonstrated that the realistic play can have as many levels of meaning, can penetrate as deeply into human experience, as that which is more obviously poetic in its language.

Of the younger American playwrights Tennessee Williams has been most often associated with the devices of the poetic dramatist. His works have been distinguished by a profusion of symbols and by deliberately lyrical turns of dialogue. Williams has shown his aversion to the realistic drama in other ways, too, as he turns his back on the structure of the well-made play and its naturalistic content. His contribution to the mid-century season was *The Rose Tattoo*, another portrait of a woman, like his other plays, but unlike them, a comic portrait.

Serafina is a Sicilian-American living somewhere along the Gulf coast near New Orleans. Her mate is a truck driver with a rose tattooed on his chest, and he is killed by the police while transporting contraband goods under a covering load of bananas. Serafina then experiences a dou-ble horror: the loss of her husband and the thought that he may have been untrue to her. Finally the combined efforts of the priest, her neighbors, another truck driver and her passionate daughter convince her that she need not wear the corpse of her husband about her neck forever.

The play finds its comedy in the most traditional places: the heroine is uncomfortable in a girdle and spends an unhappy five minutes wriggling out of it—in the approved manner of a dozen transvestian comedians. The hero woos with an excessive awkwardness like a dozen or so adolescents before him—although this lover is a grown man, his object a widow with a marriageable daughter, and the usual chair becomes a sofa which he hitches awkwardly towards her.

Roses are as thickly strewn through the evening as park-ing meters on Main Street, and their meaning is as obvious and as restricted. Roses are tattooed on the chests of Sera-fina's husband, his mistress, and the man who comes a-woo-ing. At the moment of conception a mystic rose appears on Serafina's own breast—twice. The husband's name is Ro-sario, the daughter's, Rosa delle Rose. Both the men in the heroine's life use rose oil in their hair; as a seamstress she makes up rose-colored silk into a shirt for her husband. The husband's mistress brings a bunch of roses to lay at his grave; these are snatched from her by the neighbors and used as whips to beat her with. "The rose," the new suitor solemnly declares, "is the heart of the world."

The meaning of the symbol, as it emerges from its use in the action and dialogue of the play, seems to be that the heart of the world is the sex act as performed in marriage. Out of wedlock, the sex act is associated with a goat who breaks loose off stage at apposite moments. Serafina's mo-ments of happiness are her memories of her highly satisfactory sexual relationship with her husband; her tragic moments are the result of the disclosure that she was not the only object of his endeavors. And her final triumph comes as she discovers another man as efficient and effective as the dead Rosario.

The deficiencies of the play are its structure which is spasmodic, unplanned, and undirected, and its use of poetic devices to produce an optical illusion of richness and complexity in a fundamentally shallow vision of life. The sexual union has been used by the masters of poetic drama for symbolic purposes from the beginnings of the theater, but Mr. Williams uses all of his symbolism merely to glorify the union. *The Rose Tattoo* is thus thin dramatic fare, as far as its central idea is concerned. Its great popularity with a metropolitan audience may reflect, to some extent, the popular concern about successful marital relations illustrated by the steady sale of books about "married love." Dramatically, one might hope that the devices of poetic theater might be used to penetrate the recesses of man which are not accessible to the methods of physical or psychical science. But all the symbols in *The Rose Tattoo* are related to the sex act; the sex act itself is symbolic of nothing. That audiences have found this sufficient reveals, not only the immaturity of the author, but the wilful adolescence of the applauding spectator.

The seasons following the cessation of World War II have been brightened by the plays of Tennessee Williams and Arthur Miller. Granting that an author cannot always be at the top of his form, the mid-century season may be set down as an off-year for the two dramatists who are most consistently recognized as men of greatest promise. For Philip Barry, 1950-51 brought the final realization of the promise of a quarter-century. It has often been pointed out that there were two Barrys, the man who wrote the flashing sophisticated comedy of *Holiday* and the poet who gave dramatic form to his understanding of man's fate in *Hotel Universe* and *Here Come the Clowns.* With his posthumous play, *Second Threshold,* the two Barrys become one, for this may be described as a comedy of manners in depth.[1]

As was his general practice, Barry draws his characters from the cultured, well-behaved, quietly rich. Josiah Bolton, his hero, is a career diplomat. His daughter, Miranda, the heroine, is a recent graduate of Bennington, in many ways the intellectual equal of her father. Josiah has completely withdrawn from the world—giving up his position, divorcing his wife, keeping his children at a distance; he has twice attempted suicide, and as the play begins is contemplating a third try. Miranda is about to embark on a loveless "ideal" marriage with a British diplomat of her father's generation.

Josiah is a sufficiently large character to be capable of self-analysis. At the climactic moment of the play he describes himself: a man consumed with the desire to get on, never going back to any place he had left for fear it might take something of himself away from him, who suddenly found himself alone "with the bleak, cold, crushing loneliness of the truly prideful ones." This discovery led him to seek death through a planned accident which would not leave the body on anyone's doorstep.

Miranda's ideal marriage, on the surface the union of intellectuals, is actually an attempt on her part to find a substitute for the father who has withdrawn from her. When she discovers his intent to do away with himself she is, of course, horrified and undertakes what she calls "shock therapy" in an effort to save him. She persuades the De-

[1] Barry's manuscript was revised for production by Robert E. Sherwood.

partment of State to urgently request his services, his ex-
wife to telegraph him a warm invitation to visit her, his
son, in whom he has been deeply disappointed, to give up
the theater and make another stab at the law. But Josiah is
not to be taken in by such easy gestures. If Miranda is to
save him she must do what he has refused to do, commit
suicide herself.

Against the father and daughter, Barry sets two opposite
points of view. Dr. Toby Wells, in love with Miranda, is
on hand to recommend feeling as a more effective agent
than thinking in handling the crisis. Thankful Mather, a
Bennington undergraduate and one of Barry's most de-
lightful females, is a living symbol of the acceptance of the
fact that life is good and that experiences are to be treas-
ured. It is hard to say which of the two is more effective in
achieving the happy ending of the play. Josiah's attitude
toward Thankful is at first that of ironical co-operation in a
little game. By the end of the play, however, her own enthusiasm for life, her delighted acceptance of anything that
experience offers, even her good appetite, reawaken in
Josiah some of the sensitivity he had forced into hiberna-
tion.

Dr. Wells, who is in love with Miranda, contributes
mainly to her decision. Completely aware of the nature of
Josiah's affliction, he realizes it can only be cured by love,
by feeling. Although himself a scientific man, he knows
that only an emotional act can draw Josiah back from
death. It is he who points out to Miranda that psychiatry
is not enough. "What shall it profit a man if he gain the
whole world and have not lost himself in the love of his
family?" At one point Toby tells Miranda a little modern
fable, about a woman who recovered from Spotted Fever
with the aid of aureomycin. "Wonderful stuff," he says,

"these new drugs. But in many cases, if I had to choose between them and the will to live, I'd take the old original." Yet, as if to declare his honesty, he adds a moment later, "All the same, it's nice we have both."

The construction of the play is of a piece with its theme. In the moments of high-comedy fencing, as the characters hold one another off, Barry is at his most brilliant, tapping out dialogue of the greatest economy and brittleness. But as the action progresses, as Toby and Thankful succeed in pointing out to the principals the necessity for commitment and acceptance of life, the impassioned sincerity of the speeches takes on other dimensions. Yet never does Barry descend to sentimentality. Even at their moment of reconciliation his characters remain honest; they are still cultured and intelligent, still capable of wit and irony. They are richer, broader, deeper, in their discovery of the essential importance of human values in a world governed in turn by animals and machines.

The season of 1950-51 was not very different then from the seasons that had immediately preceded it. There were a few successful plays, fewer that had a chance of revival, a number of popular entertainments, and a large number of commercial failures. In a way the failures are more interesting than the successes, for in many cases they too would have succeeded in the theater at the beginning of the century. On the other hand, *Billy Budd, The Autumn Garden* and *Second Threshold* are inconceivable in that theater. And in the differences in subject matter and form between such plays and *The Girl with the Green Eyes, Sherlock Holmes,* or *The Easiest Way* lies the measure of the growth of the American drama in half a century.

In the perverse way of the theater the mid-century season was not the distinguished affair it should have been. When the final curtains fell on the night of May 31, 1951, they signalled only the nightly ending of a commercial operation. On June first they would rise again, or in September on another show. For nothing is more certain in the theater than that something is "Coming next week" and that changes in the structure and content of plays are slow and dependent on the willingness of the audience to accept them. All final curtains in the theater are but Act Drops, ready to rise again when the setting has been changed and the players are ready to go on.

SUGGESTED READINGS

READERS WHO WISH a more extended account of the history of the American drama and the stage are advised to consult *A History of the American Drama: From the Civil War to the Present Day* by Arthur Hobson Quinn, New York, F. S. Crofts Company, 1945; or *A History of Modern Drama*, edited by Barrett H. Clark and George Freedley, New York, Appleton-Century-Crofts, Inc., 1947.

Special aspects of the history are covered in *The Provincetown,* by Helen Deutsch and Stella Hanau, New York, Farrar and Rinehart, Inc., 1931; *Arena* (The story of the Federal Theatre), by Hallie Ferguson Flanagan, New York, Duell, Sloan & Pearce, Inc., 1940; *The Fervent Years,* by Harold Clurman, New York, Alfred A. Knopf, Inc., 1945.

Critical views of the American drama from many angles may be found in volumes of collected reviews by John Mason Brown, particularly in *Broadway in Review,* New York, W. W. Norton and Company, 1940; *Matinée Tomorrow,* by Ward Morehouse, New York, McGraw Hill Book Company, 1949; *Theatre Book of the Year,* by George Jean Nathan, published annually since 1942–43; *Broadway Scrapbook,* by Brooks Atkinson, New York, Theatre Arts Books, 1947; *Immortal Shadows,* by Stark Young, New York, Charles Scribner's Sons, 1948.

Plays may be found in convenient anthologies. For the

older titles consult *American Plays,* edited by Allen Gates Halline, New York, American Book Company, 1935; *Representative American Plays from 1767 to the Present Day,* edited by Arthur Hobson Quinn, New York, The Century Company, 1917 and after. Some of the more recent plays may be read in two anthologies edited by John Gassner: *Twenty Best Plays of the Modern American Theatre,* New York, Crown Publishers, 1939, and *Best Plays of the Modern American Theatre,* 2nd Series, New York, Crown Publishers, 1947.

INDEX